RAG Generative AI

A Practical Guide to Building Custom Retrieval-Augmented Pipelines and Enhancing AI Systems.

Written by

Julie Smith

Your feedback is invaluable to me!

If you found this book helpful in any way, please take a moment to leave your review here on Amazon . Your thoughts and experiences will help other readers make informed decisions and contribute to the ongoing improvement of this work.

Table of contents

Are you ready to unlock the full potential of AI?

Imagine a world where AI can access and understand vast amounts of information, providing you with instant, accurate, and insightful responses to your queries. A world where AI can generate creative content, solve complex problems, and assist you in countless ways.

This is the power of Retrieval-Augmented Generation (RAG).

What if you could build your own RAG system?

A system that could help your business, your research, or even your personal life. A system that could understand your needs and provide tailored solutions.

This book is your guide to building custom RAG pipelines.

We'll dive deep into the technical aspects, from data preparation and embedding techniques to advanced prompt engineering and model fine-tuning. You'll learn how to leverage powerful tools and frameworks like LangChain, Haystack, and Hugging Face Transformers to create intelligent and versatile RAG systems.

But it's not just about the technology.

We'll explore the ethical implications of AI, the importance of bias mitigation, and the need for responsible AI development. You'll learn how to build systems that are fair, transparent, and accountable.

Ready to embark on this exciting journey?

Let's unlock the future of AI together.

Part I

Foundations of RAG and Generative AI

Chapter 1: Introduction to Generative AI and RAG

1.1 What is Generative AI?

Generative AI is a branch of artificial intelligence that focuses on creating new content. This content can take many forms, including text, images, music, and even video. The core idea behind generative AI is to train a model on a massive dataset of existing content, and then use that model to generate new content that is similar in style and quality to the original data.

How Does Generative AI Work?

Generative AI models learn patterns from the data they are trained on. Once trained, these models can generate new content by:

1. Predicting the Next Element: The model predicts the next element in a sequence, such as the next word in a sentence or the next pixel in an image.
2. Sampling from a Probability Distribution: The model generates content by sampling from a probability distribution over possible outputs.

Key Techniques in Generative AI

- Generative Adversarial Networks (GANs): GANs consist of two neural networks, a generator and a discriminator. The generator creates new data, while the discriminator evaluates its authenticity. This adversarial process leads to the generation of highly realistic content.
- Variational Autoencoders (VAEs): VAEs learn a latent representation of data, allowing for the generation of new data points by sampling from this latent space.

- Large Language Models (LLMs): LLMs are trained on massive amounts of text data and can generate human-quality text, translate languages, write different kinds of creative content, and answer your questions in an informative way.

Real-world Applications of Generative AI

Generative AI has a wide range of applications across various industries:

- Creative Industries: Generating art, music, and literature.
- Gaming: Creating realistic game environments and characters.
- Healthcare: Designing new drugs and analyzing medical images.
- Marketing: Creating personalized marketing content.
- Education: Developing intelligent tutoring systems and personalized learning experiences.

As generative AI continues to evolve, we can expect to see even more innovative and impactful applications in the future.

Generative AI has its roots in the early days of artificial intelligence. Let's take a journey through its evolution:

Early Beginnings (1950s-1980s)

- Markov Chains: These statistical models were used to generate text and music. While simple, they laid the foundation for more complex generative models.
- Neural Networks: Early neural networks, inspired by the human brain, were used to learn patterns in data. They were applied to tasks like image recognition and speech recognition.

The Rise of Modern Generative AI (1990s-2010s)

- Generative Adversarial Networks (GANs): Introduced in 2014, GANs revolutionized generative AI. They consist of two neural networks: a generator and a discriminator.
  - Generator: Creates new data samples.
  - Discriminator: Evaluates the realism of the generated samples.
  - Through a competitive process, the generator learns to produce increasingly realistic outputs.

Example: Generating Realistic Images

1. Training Data: A dataset of real images (e.g., faces, landscapes).
2. Generator: Creates a random image.
3. Discriminator: Evaluates the image's realism compared to real images.
4. Feedback Loop: The generator is updated based on the discriminator's feedback, aiming to create more realistic images.
5. Iterative Process: This process continues until the generator can produce highly realistic images.
- Variational Autoencoders (VAEs): VAEs are another powerful generative model. They learn a latent representation of data, allowing for the generation of new data points by sampling from this latent space.

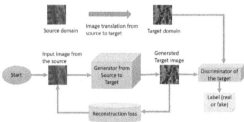

Example: Generating Handwritten Digits

1. Encoder: Maps input images (handwritten digits) to a lower-dimensional latent space.

2. Decoder: Reconstructs the original image from the latent representation.
3. Training: The model is trained to minimize the reconstruction error.
4. Generation: By sampling from the latent space, the model can generate new, realistic handwritten digits.

The Age of Large Language Models (2010s-Present)

- Large Language Models (LLMs): Trained on massive amounts of text data, LLMs can generate human-quality text, translate languages, write different kinds of creative content, and answer your questions in an informative way.

Example: GPT-3

OpenAI's GPT-3 is a state-of-the-art LLM capable of generating various creative text formats, from poems to code. It can be used for tasks like:

- Text generation: Writing articles, scripts, and code.
- Translation: Translating text between languages.
- Summarization: Condensing long texts into shorter

summaries.

These are just a few examples of the many advancements in generative AI. As technology continues to evolve, we can expect to see even more innovative and exciting applications in the future.

Generative Adversarial Networks (GANs)

How GANs Work:

1. Generator: Takes random noise as input and generates a new data sample.
2. Discriminator: Evaluates the generated sample and real data samples.
3. Training: The generator and discriminator are trained in an adversarial manner:
   - The generator aims to fool the discriminator by producing more realistic samples.
   - The discriminator aims to accurately distinguish between real and fake samples.

Real-world Example: Image Generation

- Training Data: A dataset of real images (e.g., faces, landscapes).
- Generator: Creates a random image.
- Discriminator: Evaluates the image's realism compared to real images.
- Feedback Loop: The generator is updated based on the discriminator's feedback, aiming to create more realistic images.
- Iterative Process: This process continues until the generator can produce highly realistic images.

Code Example (PyTorch):

Python

```python
import torch

import torch.nn as nn


# Define the generator and discriminator networks

class Generator(nn.Module):
```

```python
    # ...

class Discriminator(nn.Module):

    # ...


# Create instances of the generator and discriminator

generator = Generator()

discriminator = Discriminator()


# Training loop

for epoch in range(num_epochs):

    for i, (real_images, _) in enumerate(dataloader):

        # Train the discriminator

        # ...


        # Train the generator

        # ...
```

Variational Autoencoders (VAEs)

How VAEs Work:

1. Encoder: Maps input data to a latent space.
2. Decoder: Reconstructs the original data from the latent representation.
3. Training: The VAE is trained to minimize the reconstruction error and maximize the likelihood of the latent code.
4. Generation: By sampling from the latent space, the model can generate new data points.

Real-world Example: Generating Handwritten Digits

1. Encoder: Maps input images (handwritten digits) to a lower-dimensional latent space.
2. Decoder: Reconstructs the original image from the latent representation.
3. Training: The model is trained to minimize the reconstruction error.
4. Generation: By sampling from the latent space, the model can generate new, realistic handwritten digits.

Code Example (PyTorch):

Python

```python
import torch

import torch.nn as nn


# Define the encoder and decoder networks

class Encoder(nn.Module):

    # ...
```

```python
class Decoder(nn.Module):

    # ...


# Create instances of the encoder and decoder
encoder = Encoder()
decoder = Decoder()


# Training loop
for epoch in range(num_epochs):
    for i, (images, _) in enumerate(dataloader):
        # Encode the images
        z = encoder(images)

        # Decode the latent codes
        reconstructed_images = decoder(z)

        # Calculate the loss
        loss = # ...
```

```
# Update the model parameters

optimizer.zero_grad()

loss.backward()

optimizer.step()
```

Large Language Models (LLMs)

How LLMs Work:

1. Training Data: A massive dataset of text and code.
2. Transformer Architecture: LLMs use a transformer architecture, which allows them to process sequences of data efficiently.
3. Training: The model is trained to predict the next word in a sequence, given the previous words.
4. Generation: The model can generate text by iteratively predicting the next word.

Real-world Example: Text Generation

- Prompt: "Write a poem about a lonely robot."
- LLM: Generates a poem based on the prompt and its training data.

Code Example (Hugging Face Transformers):

Python

```python
from transformers import pipeline


# Load a pre-trained LLM
```

```
generator = pipeline("text-generation", model="gpt2")


# Generate text

prompt = "Write a poem about a lonely robot."

output = generator(prompt, max_length=50,
num_return_sequences=1)

print(output[0]['generated_text'])
```

These techniques are fundamental to modern generative AI,
enabling the creation of stunningly realistic and creative content.

1.2 The Limitations of Traditional Generative AI

While generative AI has made significant strides, traditional
methods still face several limitations:

Lack of Contextual Understanding

- Limited Coherence: Traditional models often struggle to
  generate coherent and contextually relevant text, especially
  when dealing with complex topics or long-form content.
- Inconsistent Quality: The quality of generated content can
  vary widely, leading to inconsistencies and errors.

Difficulty in Controlling Generation Process

- Limited Control: It can be challenging to control the specific
  content and style of generated output.

- Unpredictability: The generation process can be unpredictable, leading to unexpected and sometimes undesirable results.

Data Dependency

- Data Quality: The quality of generated content is heavily reliant on the quality and quantity of the training data.
- Bias and Fairness: Biases present in the training data can be reflected in the generated output.

Computational Cost

- Resource-Intensive: Training and running large generative models can be computationally expensive, requiring significant hardware resources.

Ethical Considerations

- Misinformation and Disinformation: Generative AI can be used to create misleading or harmful content.
- Intellectual Property: The ownership and copyright of generated content can be complex.

To address these limitations, researchers and developers are exploring innovative techniques, such as:

- Fine-tuning: Adapting pre-trained models to specific tasks and domains.
- Prompt Engineering: Carefully crafting prompts to guide the generation process.
- Reinforcement Learning: Training models to generate high-quality content through feedback.
- Ethical AI Guidelines: Developing guidelines to ensure responsible and ethical use of generative AI.

By addressing these limitations and embracing ethical considerations, we can unlock the full potential of generative AI and create more sophisticated and beneficial applications.

1.3 Introducing Retrieval-Augmented Generation (RAG)

Retrieval-Augmented Generation (RAG) is an emerging technique that combines the power of large language models (LLMs) with external knowledge sources. This approach aims to overcome the limitations of traditional generative AI models by providing them with access to relevant information at the time of generation.

How RAG Works:

1. Document Retrieval: A document retrieval system is used to identify relevant information from a knowledge base or external database.
2. Language Model Processing: The retrieved information is processed by a language model to generate text.
3. Output Generation: The language model generates text that is informed by the retrieved information, resulting in more accurate and coherent output.

Key Benefits of RAG:

- Improved Factual Accuracy: By accessing relevant information, RAG models can generate more accurate and factual text.
- Enhanced Coherence: RAG models can produce more coherent and contextually relevant text, as they are grounded in factual information.
- Reduced Hallucinations: RAG can help mitigate the issue of hallucinations, where models generate incorrect or nonsensical information.

- Increased Flexibility: RAG models can adapt to new information and domains by accessing and processing relevant knowledge.

Real-world Applications of RAG:

- Customer Service: RAG can be used to power chatbots and virtual assistants, providing more accurate and informative responses to customer queries.
- Content Creation: RAG can assist in content creation by providing relevant information and suggestions.
- Research and Analysis: RAG can help researchers and analysts by summarizing large amounts of information and identifying relevant insights.

By leveraging the power of both language models and external knowledge sources, RAG offers a promising approach to building more intelligent and informative AI systems.

Document Retrieval

Document Retrieval is the process of identifying and fetching relevant information from a large corpus of documents. This is a crucial step in RAG systems.

Key Techniques:

- Keyword Search: Simple but effective, keyword search involves matching query terms with document keywords.
- Semantic Search: Utilizes natural language processing techniques to understand the semantic meaning of queries and documents, enabling more accurate and relevant results.
- Vector Databases: These databases store documents as vectors in a high-dimensional space, allowing for efficient similarity search based on semantic similarity.

Example: Building a Document Retrieval System

1. Data Collection: Gather a corpus of documents (e.g., articles, books, research papers).
2. Preprocessing: Clean and preprocess the documents (e.g., tokenization, stemming, stop word removal).
3. Embedding: Convert documents and queries into dense vector representations using techniques like TF-IDF or word embeddings.
4. Vector Database: Store document embeddings in a vector database.
5. Query Processing: Convert user queries into vector representations.
6. Similarity Search: Use a similarity search algorithm (e.g., cosine similarity) to find the most similar documents to the query.
7. Retrieval: Retrieve the top-ranked documents and return them to the user.

Language Models

Language Models are trained on massive amounts of text data to understand and generate human language. They are a core component of RAG systems, responsible for processing and generating text.

Key Techniques:

- Transformer Architecture: A powerful neural network architecture that excels at processing sequential data, such as text.
- Pre-trained Language Models: Models like GPT-3 and BERT are pre-trained on large datasets and can be fine-tuned for specific tasks.
- Prompt Engineering: The art of crafting effective prompts to guide the language model's generation process.

Example: Using a Language Model for Text Generation

1. Prompt Engineering: Create a clear and concise prompt that specifies the desired output.
2. Model Input: Feed the prompt to the language model.
3. Text Generation: The model generates text token by token, conditioned on the previous tokens and the prompt.
4. Output: The generated text is returned as the final output.

By combining document retrieval and language models, RAG systems can access and leverage information from the real world to generate more informative and relevant responses.

RAG addresses the limitations of traditional generative AI by providing access to relevant information, improving factual accuracy, and enhancing the coherence and contextuality of generated text.

Here's a breakdown of how RAG overcomes these limitations:

1. Addressing Lack of Contextual Understanding

- Factual Accuracy: RAG systems can access and incorporate factual information from external sources, reducing the likelihood of hallucinations and generating more accurate and reliable text.
- Contextual Coherence: By referring to relevant information, RAG models can generate text that is more coherent and flows smoothly, avoiding inconsistencies and abrupt topic shifts.

2. Improving Control over Generation Process

- Prompt Engineering: RAG systems allow for more precise control over the generation process through prompt engineering. By carefully crafting prompts, users can guide the model to generate specific types of content.

- Conditioning on External Information: RAG models can be conditioned on specific documents or datasets, enabling the generation of highly targeted and relevant text.

3. Reducing Data Dependency and Bias

- Knowledge Base: RAG systems can leverage knowledge bases to access a wider range of information, reducing the reliance on a single training dataset.
- Bias Mitigation: By incorporating diverse and unbiased information sources, RAG models can help mitigate biases that may be present in training data.

Real-world Example: Customer Service Chatbot

A traditional chatbot might struggle to answer complex queries or provide accurate information. A RAG-powered chatbot, on the other hand, can access a knowledge base of product information, FAQs, and customer support documents. This enables the chatbot to provide more accurate and informative responses, improving customer satisfaction.

RAG Pipeline:

1. User Query: The user asks a question.
2. Document Retrieval: The system retrieves relevant documents from the knowledge base.
3. Language Model Processing: The language model processes the query and retrieved documents to generate a response.
4. Response Generation: The model generates a response that is informative, relevant, and addresses the user's query.

By combining the strengths of language models and document retrieval, RAG offers a powerful approach to building more intelligent and informative AI systems.

Chapter 2: Understanding Large Language Models (LLMs)

2.1 The Architecture of LLMs

Large Language Models (LLMs) are a type of artificial intelligence that can process and generate human-quality text. These models are built upon a specific neural network architecture known as the Transformer.

The Transformer Architecture

The Transformer architecture is a powerful neural network model designed to process sequential data, such as text. It consists of two main components:

1. Encoder:
    - Self-Attention Layer: This layer allows the model to weigh the importance of different parts of the input sequence. This helps the model capture long-range dependencies and contextual information.
    - Positional Encoding: This layer adds positional information to the input sequence, allowing the model to understand the order of words.
    - Feed-Forward Neural Network: This layer applies a non-linear transformation to each position in the sequence.
2. Decoder:
    - Self-Attention Layer: Similar to the encoder's self-attention layer, this layer helps the model attend to relevant parts of the generated sequence.
    - Encoder-Decoder Attention Layer: This layer allows the decoder to attend to the relevant parts of the input sequence.

○ Feed-Forward Neural Network: Similar to the encoder's feed-forward layer.

How LLMs Work

1. Tokenization: The input text is broken down into smaller units called tokens.
2. Embedding: Each token is converted into a numerical representation called an embedding.
3. Encoder-Decoder Processing: The input sequence is processed by the encoder, and the decoder generates the output sequence, token by token.
4. Decoding: The generated tokens are converted back into text.

Key Points:

- Self-Attention: This mechanism allows the model to weigh the importance of different parts of the input sequence, enabling it to capture long-range dependencies.
- Parallel Processing: The Transformer architecture allows for parallel processing of the input sequence, making it efficient for large-scale language models.
- Scalability: LLMs can be scaled up by increasing the number of layers and parameters, leading to improved performance.

By understanding the architecture of LLMs, we can gain insights into how these models are able to generate human-quality text and perform complex language tasks.

Understanding the Transformer

The Transformer architecture is a powerful neural network model designed to process sequential data, such as text. It has revolutionized the field of natural language processing, enabling the development of state-of-the-art language models.

Key Components of a Transformer:

1. Encoder:
   - Input Embedding Layer: Converts input tokens into numerical representations.
   - Positional Encoding Layer: Adds positional information to the input embeddings.
   - Encoder-Decoder Attention Layer: Allows the encoder to attend to relevant parts of the input sequence.
   - Feed-Forward Neural Network: Applies a non-linear transformation to each position in the sequence.
2. Decoder:
   - Masked Self-Attention Layer: Prevents the model from attending to future tokens during the generation process.
   - Encoder-Decoder Attention Layer: Allows the decoder to attend to relevant parts of the encoder's output.
   - Feed-Forward Neural Network: Applies a non-linear transformation to each position in the sequence.
   - Output Layer: Generates the final output token.

Step-by-Step Breakdown

1. Input Embedding:

- Convert input text into a sequence of tokens.
- Embed each token into a dense vector representation.

2. Positional Encoding:

- Add positional information to the input embeddings to indicate the relative or absolute position of each token.
- This allows the model to understand the order of words in the sequence.

3. Encoder-Decoder Attention:

- The encoder-decoder attention layer allows the decoder to attend to relevant parts of the input sequence.
- This helps the model capture long-range dependencies and generate contextually relevant output.

4. Feed-Forward Neural Network:

- Applies a non-linear transformation to each position in the sequence.
- This helps the model capture complex patterns in the data.

5. Output Layer:

- Generates the final output token, conditioned on the previous tokens and the input sequence.

Real-world Example: Machine Translation

A Transformer-based machine translation model can be trained on a large dataset of parallel text (e.g., English-French). The encoder processes the English input sentence, and the decoder generates the French translation, leveraging the attention mechanism to align words and phrases between the two languages.

Key Advantages of the Transformer Architecture:

- Parallel Processing: The Transformer architecture allows for parallel processing of the input sequence, making it efficient for large-scale models.
- Long-Range Dependencies: The self-attention mechanism enables the model to capture long-range dependencies between words, improving the quality of generated text.
- Flexibility: The Transformer architecture can be adapted to various natural language processing tasks, including text summarization, question answering, and text generation.

By understanding the Transformer architecture, we can appreciate the power and versatility of large language models.

Data for Training LLMs

To train a powerful LLM, a massive amount of text data is required. This data can come from various sources, such as:

- Books: A diverse collection of books can provide a rich source of language and knowledge.
- Articles: News articles, blog posts, and research papers offer a wealth of factual and informative text.
- Code: Code repositories like GitHub can be used to train models for code generation and understanding.
- Web Text: Web scraping can be used to collect text from websites, forums, and social media.

Training Objectives

The primary objective of LLM training is to minimize the loss function, which measures the difference between the model's predicted output and the actual target output. Common loss functions used in LLM training include:

- Cross-Entropy Loss: Measures the difference between the predicted probability distribution and the true probability distribution of the target token.
- Language Modeling Objective: Trains the model to predict the next word in a sequence, given the previous words.
- Masked Language Modeling: Randomly masks certain tokens in the input sequence and trains the model to predict the original tokens.

Fine-tuning LLMs

Fine-tuning involves taking a pre-trained LLM and adapting it to a specific task or domain. This is often done by training the model on a smaller, task-specific dataset.

Common Fine-tuning Techniques:

- Task-Specific Fine-tuning: Train the model on a dataset of task-specific examples (e.g., question-answer pairs, code snippets).
- Prompt-Based Learning: Provide the model with specific prompts to guide its generation process.
- Reinforcement Learning from Human Feedback (RLHF): Train the model to generate text that aligns with human preferences.

Example: Fine-tuning a Language Model for Text Summarization

1. Pre-trained Model: Start with a pre-trained language model like GPT-3.
2. Task-Specific Dataset: Collect a dataset of articles and their corresponding summaries.
3. Fine-tuning: Train the model on the summarization dataset, adjusting the model's parameters to improve its ability to generate concise and informative summaries.
4. Prompt Engineering: Use prompts like "Summarize the following text:" to guide the model's generation process.

By carefully selecting training data, optimizing the training process, and fine-tuning the model, researchers and developers can create powerful LLMs capable of a wide range of language tasks.

2.2 Capabilities and Limitations of LLMs

Large Language Models (LLMs) have demonstrated impressive capabilities, but they also have limitations that need to be considered.

Capabilities of LLMs

- Text Generation: LLMs can generate human-quality text, including articles, poems, scripts, and code.

- Translation: They can translate text from one language to another with high accuracy.
- Summarization: LLMs can condense long texts into shorter summaries.
- Question Answering: They can answer questions based on a given context or knowledge base.
- Code Generation: LLMs can generate code snippets or even entire programs.

Limitations of LLMs

- Factual Accuracy: LLMs can sometimes generate incorrect or misleading information, especially when the training data is biased or inaccurate.
- Lack of Common Sense: LLMs may struggle with tasks that require common sense or real-world knowledge.
- Sensitivity to Prompting: The quality of the generated text can be highly dependent on the prompt. Poorly crafted prompts can lead to suboptimal results.
- Computational Cost: Training and running large language models can be computationally expensive, requiring significant hardware resources.
- Ethical Concerns: LLMs can be used to generate harmful or misleading content, raising ethical concerns about their use.

Mitigating Limitations:

To address these limitations, researchers are exploring various techniques:

- Improved Training Data: Using high-quality, diverse, and unbiased training data.
- Advanced Training Techniques: Employing techniques like reinforcement learning to fine-tune models.
- Prompt Engineering: Carefully crafting prompts to guide the model's generation process.

- Fact-Checking and Verification: Implementing mechanisms to verify the accuracy of generated text.
- Ethical Guidelines: Developing guidelines for the responsible use of LLMs.

By understanding the capabilities and limitations of LLMs, we can harness their potential while mitigating their risks.

Text Generation

Task: Given a prompt, generate a coherent and relevant piece of text.

Example:

- Prompt: "Write a poem about a lonely robot."
- Generated Text:
    - A lonely robot, circuits humming low, Dreams of a world it's yet to know. In a digital dawn, a solitary sight, Yearning for warmth, a guiding light.

Code Example (Using Hugging Face Transformers):

Python

```python
from transformers import pipeline


generator = pipeline("text-generation", model="gpt2")


prompt = "Write a poem about a lonely robot."
```

```
output = generator(prompt, max_length=50,
num_return_sequences=1)

print(output[0]['generated_text'])
```

Text Summarization

Task: Condense a long text into a shorter summary.

Example:

- Input Text: A lengthy news article about climate change.
- Generated Summary: A concise summary highlighting the key points of the article.

Code Example (Using Hugging Face Transformers):

Python

```
from transformers import pipeline


summarizer = pipeline("summarization")


text = "A long text to be summarized..."

summary = summarizer(text)

print(summary[0]['summary_text'])
```

Machine Translation

Task: Translate text from one language to another.

Example:

- Input Text: "Hello, how are you?" (English)
- Generated Translation: "Bonjour, comment allez-vous ?" (French)

Code Example (Using Hugging Face Transformers):

Python

```python
from transformers import pipeline


translator = pipeline("translation_en_fr")


text = "Hello, how are you?"

translation = translator(text)

print(translation[0]['translation_text'])
```

Real-World Applications:

- Content Creation: Generating product descriptions, blog posts, and marketing copy.
- Language Learning: Translating text to facilitate language learning.
- Information Retrieval: Summarizing lengthy documents to extract key information.
- Customer Service: Generating automated responses to customer inquiries.

By understanding the capabilities of LLMs in these areas, we can leverage their potential to automate tasks, improve productivity, and create innovative applications.

While LLMs have made significant strides in generating text and understanding language, they still face limitations in complex reasoning and problem-solving tasks. However, recent advancements have shown promising results in these areas.

Reasoning

LLMs can be used to perform various reasoning tasks, such as:

- Logical Reasoning: Deductive and inductive reasoning.
- Causal Reasoning: Understanding cause-effect relationships.
- Analogical Reasoning: Identifying similarities and differences between concepts.

Example: Logical Reasoning

- Prompt: "If all birds can fly and a penguin is a bird, can a penguin fly?"
- Expected Response: "No, penguins cannot fly."

Problem-Solving

LLMs can be applied to solve various problems, including:

- Question Answering: Answering questions based on a given context.
- Text Summarization: Condensing long texts into shorter summaries.
- Text Generation: Generating creative text formats, from poems to code.

Example: Question Answering

- Context: A news article about climate change.
- Question: "What are the main causes of climate change?"
- Expected Response: The model should identify the relevant sections of the article and extract the main causes, such as greenhouse gas emissions from human activities.

Limitations and Challenges:

- Factual Accuracy: LLMs can sometimes generate incorrect or misleading information, especially when the training data is biased or inaccurate.
- Common Sense Reasoning: LLMs may struggle with tasks that require common sense or real-world knowledge.
- Complex Reasoning: Complex reasoning tasks, such as multi-step reasoning and planning, can be challenging for LLMs.

Addressing Limitations:

To improve the reasoning and problem-solving capabilities of LLMs, researchers are exploring various techniques, such as:

- Knowledge Base Integration: Incorporating knowledge bases and external information sources into the training process.
- Reinforcement Learning: Training LLMs to make decisions based on rewards and penalties.
- Prompt Engineering: Carefully crafting prompts to guide the model's reasoning process.
- Hierarchical Reasoning: Breaking down complex problems into smaller, more manageable subproblems.

By addressing these limitations and leveraging advanced techniques, LLMs can become more powerful tools for reasoning and problem-solving.

Hallucinations

Hallucinations occur when an LLM generates text that is not factually accurate or relevant to the prompt. This can happen due to various reasons, including:

- Lack of Training Data: If the model hasn't been trained on sufficient data, it may generate incorrect or nonsensical text.
- Overfitting: Overfitting can lead the model to memorize the training data rather than learning underlying patterns.
- Prompt Engineering: Poorly designed prompts can confuse the model and lead to hallucinations.

Example:

- Prompt: "Tell me about the capital of France."
- Hallucination: The model might generate incorrect information, such as "The capital of France is Berlin."

Bias

LLMs can exhibit biases that are present in the training data. These biases can lead to unfair or discriminatory outputs.

Types of Bias:

- Representation Bias: The model may underrepresent certain groups or perspectives.
- Algorithmic Bias: The model's algorithms may inherently favor certain groups.
- Dataset Bias: The training data may contain biases, which are then reflected in the model's outputs.

Example:

- Biased Training Data: If a language model is trained on a dataset that primarily features male authors, it may generate text that reinforces gender stereotypes.

Mitigating Hallucinations and Bias:

To address these issues, several techniques can be employed:

1. High-Quality Training Data: Using diverse and unbiased datasets can help mitigate bias.
2. Careful Prompt Engineering: Well-crafted prompts can guide the model towards accurate and unbiased outputs.
3. Fact-Checking and Verification: Implementing mechanisms to verify the accuracy of generated text.
4. Fairness and Bias Mitigation Techniques: Employing techniques like fair representation and adversarial debiasing.
5. Human Oversight: Human review and feedback can help identify and correct biases.

By understanding and addressing these limitations, we can develop more reliable and unbiased LLMs.

Part II

Building Custom RAG Pipelines

Chapter 3: Document Retrieval and Indexing

3.1 The Role of Document Retrieval in RAG

Document Retrieval is a fundamental component of Retrieval-Augmented Generation (RAG) systems. It involves identifying and fetching relevant information from a large corpus of documents. This process is crucial for RAG systems to access and leverage external knowledge to improve the quality and accuracy of their generated output.

Key Roles of Document Retrieval in RAG:

1. Providing Contextual Information:
   - By retrieving relevant documents, RAG systems can provide additional context to the language model, enabling it to generate more informative and accurate responses.
   - For example, when answering a query about a specific event, a RAG system can retrieve news articles, research papers, or historical documents related to the event.
2. Enhancing Factual Accuracy:
   - Access to a vast knowledge base allows RAG systems to verify information and avoid generating incorrect or misleading content.
   - By cross-referencing information from multiple sources, RAG systems can improve the reliability of their output.
3. Improving Coherence and Relevance:
   - Document retrieval helps ensure that the generated text is coherent and relevant to the query.

- By identifying and incorporating relevant information, RAG systems can produce more focused and informative responses.
4. Enabling Knowledge-Grounded Generation:
   - RAG systems can use retrieved documents to generate text that is grounded in specific knowledge.
   - This is particularly useful for tasks like summarization, question answering, and creative writing.

In essence, document retrieval serves as the backbone of RAG systems, providing the necessary information for language models to generate high-quality and informative output.

3.2 Vector Databases: An Overview

Vector databases are specialized databases designed to store and retrieve data represented as vectors. These databases are particularly well-suited for handling large-scale similarity search and recommendation tasks. In the context of RAG systems, vector databases are used to efficiently store and retrieve relevant documents based on their semantic similarity to a query.

Key Concepts:

- Vector Embeddings: Text, images, or other types of data can be transformed into dense vector representations using techniques like word embeddings or image embeddings. These vectors capture the semantic and syntactic meaning of the data.
- Similarity Search: Vector databases use similarity search algorithms (e.g., cosine similarity, Euclidean distance) to find the most similar vectors to a query vector. This allows for efficient retrieval of relevant documents.

Popular Vector Databases:

- Faiss: Developed by Facebook AI Research, Faiss is a library for efficient similarity search and clustering of dense vectors.
- Milvus: An open-source vector database designed for scalable similarity search and analytics.
- Pinecone: A cloud-based vector database that offers a user-friendly interface and advanced features like hybrid search and filtering.

How Vector Databases Work in RAG Systems:

1. Document Embedding: Documents are converted into dense vector representations using techniques like BERT or Sentence-Transformers.
2. Vector Database Indexing: The document embeddings are indexed in a vector database, creating a searchable index.
3. Query Embedding: A user's query is also converted into a vector representation.
4. Similarity Search: The query vector is compared to the document vectors in the database, and the most similar documents are retrieved.
5. Language Model Processing: The retrieved documents are processed by a language model to generate a response.

By leveraging vector databases, RAG systems can efficiently retrieve relevant information from large-scale document collections, enabling them to generate more accurate and informative responses.

Faiss

Faiss is a library developed by Facebook AI Research for efficient similarity search and clustering of dense vectors. It's particularly well-suited for large-scale datasets and offers a variety of algorithms for approximate nearest neighbor search.

Key Features:

- Efficient Similarity Search: Faiss provides various algorithms for efficient similarity search, including IndexIVFFlat, IndexHNSW, and IndexPQ.
- GPU Acceleration: It supports GPU acceleration for faster search and training.
- Scalability: Faiss can handle large-scale datasets and can be scaled to distributed environments.

Code Example:

Python

```python
import faiss


# Create a 10-dimensional index

dimension = 10

index = faiss.IndexFlatL2(dimension)


# Generate some random vectors

vectors = np.random.rand(1000,
dimension).astype(np.float32)


# Add vectors to the index

index.add(vectors)


# Query the index
```

```python
query_vector = np.random.rand(dimension).astype(np.float32)

distances, indices = index.search(query_vector, k=5)
```

Milvus

Milvus is an open-source vector database designed for scalable similarity search and analytics. It offers a variety of features, including hybrid search, filtering, and time-series data support.

Key Features:

- Hybrid Search: Milvus supports both exact and approximate nearest neighbor search.
- Scalability: It can handle large-scale datasets and can be scaled to distributed environments.
- Flexibility: Milvus supports various data types, including vectors, text, and time-series data.

Code Example:

Python

```python
import pymilvus


# Connect to the Milvus server

collection_name = "my_collection"

dimension = 10
```

```
# Create a new collection

collection = pymilvus.Collection(collection_name,
schema=schema)


# Insert vectors

vectors = np.random.rand(1000,
dimension).astype(np.float32)

collection.insert(vectors)


# Search the collection

search_params = {"metric_type": "L2", "params":
{"nprobe": 10}}

search_results = collection.search(vectors[:10],
search_params)
```

Pinecone

Pinecone is a cloud-based vector database that offers a
user-friendly interface and advanced features like hybrid search
and filtering. It's well-suited for real-time applications and can be
easily integrated into existing applications.

Key Features:

- Hybrid Search: Pinecone supports both exact and
  approximate nearest neighbor search.
- Filtering: Allows filtering results based on metadata.

- Time-Series Support: Can handle time-series data and perform time-based queries.

Code Example:

Python

```python
import pinecone


# Initialize the Pinecone client

pinecone.init(api_key="YOUR_API_KEY",
environment="us-west1-gcp")


# Create a new index

index_name = "my-index"

dimension = 10

metric = "cosine"

index = pinecone.Index(index_name,
dimension=dimension, metric=metric)


# Insert vectors

vectors = [

    [0.1, 0.2, 0.3],

    [0.4, 0.5, 0.6],
```

```
    # ...

]

ids = ["doc1", "doc2", ...]

index.upsert(vectors=vectors, ids=ids, meta={"source":
"my_source"})


# Query the index

query_vector = [0.2, 0.3, 0.4]

results = index.query(vector=query_vector, top_k=5)
```

By leveraging these vector databases, RAG systems can efficiently
retrieve relevant information from large-scale document
collections, enabling them to generate more accurate and
informative responses.

TF-IDF (Term Frequency-Inverse Document Frequency)

TF-IDF is a technique used to weigh the importance of words in a
document relative to a collection of documents. It helps to identify
the most relevant documents to a given query.

Steps:

1. Term Frequency (TF): Calculate the frequency of each term
   in a document.
2. Inverse Document Frequency (IDF): Calculate the inverse
   document frequency of each term, which measures how rare
   a term is in the document collection.

3. TF-IDF Score: Multiply the TF and IDF scores for each term to get the TF-IDF score.

Example:

Consider a collection of documents about cats and dogs. The word "cat" might appear frequently in documents about cats, but less frequently in documents about dogs. Therefore, the TF-IDF score for "cat" would be higher in cat-related documents.

BM25 (Okapi BM25)

BM25 is another popular technique for information retrieval. It improves upon TF-IDF by considering factors like document length and query length.

Key Factors:

- Term Frequency: The frequency of a term in a document.
- Document Length: The length of the document.
- Average Document Length: The average length of documents in the collection.
- Query Term Weight: The weight of the query term.

Example:

A longer document with a higher frequency of a query term might be ranked higher than a shorter document with the same term frequency.

Embeddings

Embeddings are dense vector representations of words, phrases, or documents. They capture semantic and syntactic information, allowing for more sophisticated similarity search.

Types of Embeddings:

- Word Embeddings: Represent individual words as vectors.

- Sentence Embeddings: Represent entire sentences or paragraphs as vectors.
- Document Embeddings: Represent entire documents as vectors.

Example:

The word "cat" and the word "dog" might be represented by similar vectors because they are semantically related.

Code Example (Using Scikit-learn):

Python

```python
from sklearn.feature_extraction.text import TfidfVectorizer


# Sample documents

documents = [

    "This is the first document.",

    "This document is the second document.",

    "And the third one, just like the first."

]


# Create a TF-IDF vectorizer

vectorizer = TfidfVectorizer()
```

```
# Fit and transform the documents

X = vectorizer.fit_transform(documents)


# Print the TF-IDF matrix

print(X.toarray())
```

By understanding these indexing techniques, we can effectively retrieve relevant documents from large-scale collections and improve the performance of RAG systems.

3.3 Building a Document Index

Building a document index is a crucial step in creating a robust RAG system. It involves preprocessing documents, creating embeddings, and storing them in a vector database.

Steps Involved:

1. Data Collection and Preprocessing:
    - Data Sources: Gather documents from various sources like websites, PDFs, or databases.
    - Cleaning and Preprocessing: Clean the text by removing stop words, punctuation, and special characters. Tokenize the text into words or sentences.
    - Normalization: Normalize the text by converting words to their root form (e.g., stemming or lemmatization).
2. Document Embedding:
    - Choose an Embedding Model: Select a suitable embedding model, such as BERT, RoBERTa, or

Sentence-Transformers, based on the specific use case and computational resources.

- ○ Embed Documents: Convert each document into a dense vector representation using the chosen embedding model. This vector captures the semantic and syntactic meaning of the document.

3. Vector Database Indexing:
   - ○ Choose a Vector Database: Select a suitable vector database, such as Faiss, Milvus, or Pinecone.
   - ○ Index Creation: Create an index in the vector database to efficiently store and search the document embeddings.
   - ○ Insert Embeddings: Insert the document embeddings into the index, along with metadata such as document titles, URLs, and creation dates.

Example:

Let's consider a scenario where we want to build a document index for a collection of news articles.

1. Data Collection: Gather news articles from various sources.
2. Preprocessing: Clean the text by removing stop words, punctuation, and converting text to lowercase.
3. Embedding: Use a pre-trained language model like BERT to generate embeddings for each article.
4. Vector Database Indexing: Create a vector database index and insert the article embeddings, along with their corresponding URLs and publication dates.

Code Example (Using Sentence-Transformers and Faiss):

Python

```python
from sentence_transformers import
SentenceTransformer
```

```python
import faiss

# Load a pre-trained sentence transformer model
model = SentenceTransformer('all-MiniLM-L6-v2')

# Embed the documents
document_embeddings = model.encode(documents)

# Create a Faiss index
dimension = document_embeddings.shape[1]
index = faiss.IndexFlatL2(dimension)
index.add(document_embeddings)

# Query the index
query_embedding = model.encode(["What is the capital of France?"])[0]
distances, indices = index.search(query_embedding, k=5)

# Retrieve the top 5 most similar documents
```

```
for i in indices[o]:

  print(documents[i])
```

By building an effective document index, RAG systems can efficiently retrieve relevant information and improve the quality of their generated output.

Data preparation and cleaning are crucial steps in building a robust document index. These steps ensure that the data is clean, consistent, and suitable for further processing.

Steps Involved:

1. Data Collection:
   - Identify Sources: Determine the sources of your documents, such as websites, PDFs, or databases.
   - Gather Data: Collect the relevant documents and store them in a suitable format (e.g., text files, PDF files).
2. Data Cleaning:
   - Remove Noise: Remove any noise or irrelevant information from the documents, such as advertisements, headers, or footers.
   - Handle Missing Data: Identify and handle missing data, either by removing it or imputing missing values.
   - Correct Errors: Correct any errors in the text, such as typos or inconsistencies.
3. Text Normalization:
   - Tokenization: Break down the text into individual words or tokens.
   - Lowercasing: Convert all text to lowercase to reduce variations.

- Stop Word Removal: Remove common words that don't add much meaning (e.g., "the," "and," "of").
- Stemming or Lemmatization: Reduce words to their root form (e.g., "running" -> "run").

Code Example (Using Python and NLTK):

Python

```
import nltk

from nltk.corpus import stopwords

from nltk.stem import PorterStemmer


# Download NLTK data

nltk.download('stopwords')

nltk.download('punkt')


# Sample text

text = "This is a sample text for cleaning and preprocessing."


# Tokenization

tokens = nltk.word_tokenize(text)
```

```python
# Lowercasing

tokens = [token.lower() for token in tokens]


# Stop word removal

stop_words = set(stopwords.words('english'))

filtered_tokens = [token for token in tokens if token not
in stop_words]


# Stemming

stemmer = PorterStemmer()

stemmed_tokens = [stemmer.stem(token) for token in
filtered_tokens]


print(stemmed_tokens)
```

Real-World Example:

Imagine you're building a document index for a collection of research papers. You might need to clean the text by removing headers, footers, and references. You would also need to normalize the text by converting it to lowercase and removing stop words.

By following these steps, you can ensure that your document index is accurate, efficient, and effective.

Embeddings are dense vector representations of words, sentences, or documents. They capture semantic and syntactic information, allowing for more sophisticated similarity search.

Steps Involved:

1. Choose an Embedding Model:
    - Pre-trained Models: Use pre-trained models like BERT, RoBERTa, or Sentence-Transformers, which are trained on massive amounts of text data.
    - Custom Models: Train a custom model on your specific dataset if you have a large amount of domain-specific data.
2. Prepare the Text:
    - Tokenization: Break down the text into tokens (words or subwords).
    - Preprocessing: Clean the text by removing stop words, punctuation, and other irrelevant information.
3. Generate Embeddings:
    - Input the Text: Feed the preprocessed text into the embedding model.
    - Obtain Embeddings: The model will output a dense vector representation for each input text.

Code Example (Using Sentence-Transformers):

Python

```python
from sentence_transformers import
SentenceTransformer



# Load a pre-trained sentence transformer model

model = SentenceTransformer('all-MiniLM-L6-v2')
```

```
# Sample text

texts = ["This is a sample sentence.", "Another sentence
for embedding."]


# Generate embeddings

embeddings = model.encode(texts)


print(embeddings)
```

Real-World Example:

Imagine you're building a search engine for a knowledge base of
scientific articles. You can use a pre-trained language model like
BERT to generate embeddings for each article. When a user
searches for a query, the query is also embedded, and the most
similar articles are retrieved based on the cosine similarity
between the query embedding and the document embeddings.

Key Considerations:

- Embedding Dimensionality: The dimensionality of the
  embeddings affects the performance of the model.
  Higher-dimensional embeddings can capture more complex
  relationships, but they may also require more
  computational resources.
- Model Choice: The choice of embedding model depends on
  the specific task and the size of the dataset. Pre-trained

models are often a good starting point, but fine-tuning them on a domain-specific dataset can improve performance.
- Computational Resources: Generating embeddings can be computationally intensive, especially for large datasets and complex models. Consider using GPUs or cloud-based computing resources to accelerate the process.

By effectively creating embeddings, you can improve the accuracy and efficiency of your document retrieval system.

Once we have generated embeddings for our documents, the next step is to store them in a vector database. This allows for efficient similarity search and retrieval.

Steps Involved:

1. Choose a Vector Database: Select a suitable vector database, such as Faiss, Milvus, or Pinecone, based on your specific needs and computational resources.
2. Create an Index: Create an index in the vector database to efficiently store and search the embeddings.
3. Insert Embeddings: Insert the document embeddings into the index, along with metadata such as document titles, URLs, and creation dates.

Code Example (Using Faiss):

Python

```
import faiss


# Create a 10-dimensional index

dimension = 10
```

```
index = faiss.IndexFlatL2(dimension)


# Generate some random vectors

vectors = np.random.rand(1000,
dimension).astype(np.float32)


# Add vectors to the index

index.add(vectors)


# Query the index

query_vector =
np.random.rand(dimension).astype(np.float32)

distances, indices = index.search(query_vector, k=5)
```

Real-World Example:

Imagine you have a large collection of product descriptions. You can create embeddings for each product description and store them in a vector database. When a user searches for a product, the query is also embedded, and the most similar products are retrieved based on the cosine similarity between the query embedding and the product embeddings.

Key Considerations:

- Indexing Efficiency: Choose an appropriate indexing technique (e.g., HNSW, IVFFlat) to optimize search performance.
- Scalability: Consider the scalability of the vector database, especially for large datasets.
- Data Privacy and Security: Implement appropriate security measures to protect sensitive data stored in the vector database.

By effectively storing embeddings in a vector database, you can create efficient and scalable RAG systems.

Chapter 4: Prompt Engineering for RAG

4.1 The Art of Prompt Design

Prompt engineering is the process of crafting effective prompts to guide language models in generating desired outputs. In the context of RAG systems, prompt design plays a crucial role in shaping the quality and relevance of the generated responses.

Key Principles of Prompt Design:

1. Clarity and Specificity:
   - Clearly articulate the desired output.
   - Provide specific instructions and constraints.
   - Avoid ambiguity and vagueness.
2. Contextual Relevance:
   - Incorporate relevant context and background information.
   - Use keywords and phrases that are relevant to the topic.
   - Provide specific examples or use cases.
3. Instructional Phrasing:
   - Use clear and concise instructions.
   - Employ specific verbs and action words.
   - Guide the model towards the desired output format.
4. Iterative Refinement:
   - Experiment with different prompts to find the optimal formulation.
   - Analyze the generated output and make adjustments to the prompt.
   - Continuously refine the prompt to improve the quality of the results.

Example Prompt:

Prompt: "Write a product description for a new AI-powered writing assistant that can help users generate creative text formats, from poems to code."

Improved Prompt:

> Prompt: "Write a concise and compelling product description for an AI writing assistant that can generate high-quality content, such as blog posts, social media posts, and email copy. Highlight the tool's ability to assist users with creative writing tasks, including poetry and code generation."

By following these principles, you can create effective prompts that guide language models to generate high-quality and relevant outputs.

Additional Tips:

- Break Down Complex Tasks: For complex tasks, break down the prompt into smaller, more manageable subtasks.
- Provide Examples: Include examples of the desired output to help the model understand the expected format and style.
- Use Specific Language: Use specific language and avoid vague terms.
- Experiment and Iterate: Don't be afraid to experiment with different prompts and see what works best.

By mastering the art of prompt engineering, you can unlock the full potential of RAG systems and generate truly impressive results.

Prompt engineering involves crafting effective prompts to guide language models towards desired outputs. A well-structured prompt can significantly improve the quality and relevance of the generated text.

Common Prompt Structures:

1. Direct Instruction:
   - Example: "Write a poem about a lonely robot."
   - Explanation: This straightforward approach provides a clear and concise instruction.
2. Question-Answer Format:
   - Example: "What is the capital of France?"
   - Explanation: This format is suitable for fact-based queries.
3. Storytelling:
   - Example: "Write a short story about a robot who dreams of becoming a chef."
   - Explanation: This format encourages creative and imaginative text generation.
4. Comparative Analysis:
   - Example: "Compare and contrast the benefits and drawbacks of electric cars and gasoline cars."
   - Explanation: This format requires the model to analyze and synthesize information.
5. Role-Playing:
   - Example: "You are a knowledgeable AI assistant. A user asks, 'What is the meaning of life?' Provide a thoughtful and insightful response."
   - Explanation: This format can be used to create more engaging and personalized interactions.

Prompt Templates:

Basic Template:

Prompt: {instruction}

Contextual Template:

Prompt: {context}

Instruction: {instruction}

Step-by-Step Template:

Prompt:

1. {Step 1}

2. {Step 2}

3. ...

Instruction: Continue the sequence.

Real-world Example:

Imagine you're building a customer service chatbot. You can use prompt engineering to create effective prompts for different scenarios:

- Product Inquiry: "Provide a detailed product description for the 'Product X' model, highlighting its key features and benefits."
- Troubleshooting: "Guide the user through troubleshooting steps for common issues with 'Product Y.'"
- Order Status: "Check the order status for order number '12345'."

By understanding the different prompt structures and templates, you can effectively guide language models to generate high-quality and relevant outputs.

Prompt engineering is an art that requires careful consideration of several best practices:

1. Be Specific and Clear

- Avoid Ambiguity: Use clear and concise language to avoid misunderstandings.
- Provide Context: If necessary, provide additional context or background information.
- Set Expectations: Clearly define the desired output format and length.

Example:

- Vague Prompt: "Write something about a cat."
- Specific Prompt: "Write a short story about a cat who dreams of becoming an astronaut."

2. Break Down Complex Tasks

- Divide and Conquer: For complex tasks, break them down into smaller, more manageable subtasks.
- Sequential Prompts: Use a series of prompts to guide the model through the process step-by-step.

Example:

- Complex Prompt: "Write a comprehensive report on the impact of climate change on global food security."
- Broken-Down Prompts:
    1. "Summarize the key points of climate change."
    2. "Discuss the potential impacts of climate change on agriculture."

3. "Analyze the potential consequences of food shortages on global economies."

3. Experiment and Iterate

- Test Different Prompts: Try different phrasing and structures to see what works best.
- Analyze the Output: Evaluate the quality of the generated text and identify areas for improvement.
- Refine the Prompt: Adjust the prompt based on the analysis of the output.

Example: If the model consistently generates irrelevant or low-quality text, try providing more specific instructions or examples.

4. Use System Messages

- Set the Stage: Use system messages to establish the desired tone, style, or perspective.
- Provide Guidelines: Give the model explicit instructions on how to format the output.

Example:

- System Message: "You are a knowledgeable and helpful AI assistant. Please provide clear and concise answers to user queries."

5. Leverage Chain-of-Thought Prompting

- Break Down Reasoning: Encourage the model to break down complex reasoning into smaller steps.
- Guide the Thought Process: Provide intermediate steps or thought processes to help the model arrive at the correct answer.

Example:

- Prompt: "How many hours are in a year?"
- Chain-of-Thought Prompt: "A year has 365 days. A day has 24 hours. So, 365 days * 24 hours/day = ..."

By following these best practices, you can effectively harness the power of language models and create high-quality, relevant, and creative text.

Prompt optimization involves fine-tuning prompts to achieve the best possible results from language models. Here are some techniques to optimize your prompts:

1. Iterative Refinement

- Start with a Basic Prompt: Begin with a simple, direct prompt.
- Analyze the Output: Evaluate the generated text for accuracy, relevance, and coherence.
- Refine the Prompt: Adjust the prompt by adding more specific instructions, examples, or constraints.

Example:

- Initial Prompt: "Write a poem about a robot."
- Refined Prompt: "Write a haiku about a lonely robot exploring a distant planet."

2. Prompt Engineering Techniques

- Few-Shot Learning: Provide a few examples of desired output to guide the model.
- Zero-Shot Learning: Use natural language instructions to guide the model without specific examples.
- Chain-of-Thought Prompting: Break down complex tasks into smaller, more manageable steps.

Example:

- Few-Shot Learning:

- Prompt: "Translate the following English sentence into French: 'Hello, how are you?'" Example 1: English: "I love cats." French: "J'aime les chats." Example 2: English: "She is a doctor." French: "Elle est médecin." Prompt: "Translate the following English sentence into French: 'What is your name?'"

3. Prompt Engineering Tools

- Prompt Libraries: Utilize pre-built prompt libraries that offer a variety of templates and examples.
- Prompt Engineering Tools: Employ specialized tools to help you create and optimize prompts.

Example:

- A prompt engineering tool might suggest different ways to phrase a prompt or provide examples of effective prompts for a specific task.

4. Experimentation and Iteration

- Test Different Prompts: Try different phrasing and structures to see what works best.
- Analyze the Output: Evaluate the generated text for quality and relevance.
- Refine the Prompt: Adjust the prompt based on the analysis of the output.

By following these techniques, you can optimize your prompts to achieve better results from language models. Remember, prompt engineering is an iterative process, and continuous experimentation is key to finding the best approach.

4.2 Prompting for Different RAG Tasks

Prompt engineering is crucial for effectively utilizing RAG systems for various tasks. By crafting precise prompts, we can guide the model to generate desired outputs. Here are some common RAG tasks and prompt engineering techniques:

1. Question Answering

- Direct Question: "What is the capital of France?"
- Contextual Question: "Given the following text about French history, what is the capital of France?"
- Comparative Question: "Compare and contrast the French Revolution and the American Revolution."

2. Text Summarization

- Specific Summary: "Summarize the key points of the following article in 50 words."
- Creative Summary: "Write a poem summarizing the main ideas of the following article."

3. Creative Writing

- Storytelling: "Write a short story about a robot who dreams of becoming a chef."
- Poetry: "Write a haiku about the beauty of nature."
- Script Writing: "Write a short script for a comedy sketch about a person who is allergic to technology."

4. Code Generation

- Specific Task: "Write a Python function to calculate the factorial of a number."
- Code Explanation: "Explain the following code snippet in plain English: def factorial(n): ..."

- Code Debugging: "Find and fix the errors in the following Python code: def ..."

5. Translation

- Direct Translation: "Translate 'Hello, how are you?' into Spanish."
- Contextual Translation: "Translate the following sentence, considering the cultural context: 'It's raining cats and dogs.'"

Key Considerations for Prompting:

- Clarity and Specificity: Use clear and concise language to avoid ambiguity.
- Contextual Relevance: Provide relevant context to guide the model's generation.
- Desired Output Format: Specify the desired output format (e.g., text, code, summary).
- Level of Detail: Adjust the level of detail required in the response.
- Ethical Considerations: Be mindful of potential biases and harmful outputs.

By mastering the art of prompt engineering, you can unlock the full potential of RAG systems and achieve impressive results.

Prompt engineering for question answering involves crafting clear and concise queries that guide the language model to provide accurate and informative responses.

Steps Involved:

1. Identify the Question: Clearly articulate the question you want to ask.
2. Provide Context (Optional): If necessary, provide additional context or background information.

3. Specify the Desired Output Format: Indicate the desired
    format of the answer (e.g., concise, detailed, bulleted list).

Example:

Simple Question:

- Prompt: "What is the capital of France?"
- Expected Response: "Paris"

Contextual Question:

- Prompt: "Given the following text about French history,
  what was the capital of France during the reign of Louis
  XIV?"
- Text: [Insert relevant historical text]
- Expected Response: "Paris"

Complex Question:

- Prompt: "Compare and contrast the French Revolution and
  the American Revolution, focusing on their causes, key
  events, and outcomes."
- Expected Response: A detailed comparison of the two
  revolutions, highlighting similarities and differences.

Code Example:

Python

```
from transformers import pipeline


# Load a pre-trained question-answering model

question_answerer = pipeline("question-answering")
```

```python
# Define the context and question

context = """

... (relevant text) ...

"""

question = "What is the capital of France?"


# Get the answer

answer = question_answerer(question=question,
context=context)

print(answer['answer'])
```

Real-world Applications:

- Customer Service Chatbots: Answering customer inquiries.
- Search Engines: Improving search results by providing more relevant and informative answers.
- Educational Tools: Answering student questions and providing explanations.

By following these steps and understanding the nuances of prompt engineering, you can effectively use RAG systems to answer a wide range of questions.

Prompt engineering for text summarization involves crafting clear and concise instructions to guide the language model in generating concise and informative summaries.

Steps Involved:

1. Provide the Text: Present the text that you want to summarize.
2. Specify the Desired Length: Indicate the desired length of the summary (e.g., 100 words, 5 sentences).
3. Set the Level of Detail: Determine the level of detail required in the summary (e.g., high-level overview, detailed summary).

Example:

Basic Summarization:

- Prompt: "Summarize the following text in 50 words."
- Text: [Insert a lengthy article or document]
- Expected Output: A concise summary of the main points.

Creative Summarization:

- Prompt: "Write a poem summarizing the key ideas of the following scientific paper."
- Text: [Insert a scientific paper]
- Expected Output: A poem that captures the essence of the paper.

Code Example:

Python

```python
from transformers import pipeline



# Load a pre-trained summarization model

summarizer = pipeline("summarization")



# Text to be summarized
```

```
text = "This is a very long text that needs to be
summarized..."
```

```
# Generate a summary

summary = summarizer(text, max_length=100,
min_length=30)

print(summary[0]['summary_text'])
```

Real-world Applications:

- News Aggregation: Summarizing news articles to provide concise overviews.
- Research Paper Summarization: Quickly understanding the key points of academic papers.
- Document Analysis: Summarizing lengthy reports or legal documents.

By effectively prompting language models, you can generate accurate and informative summaries that save time and effort.

Prompt engineering for creative writing involves crafting imaginative and inspiring prompts to stimulate the language model's creativity.

Steps Involved:

1. Set the Scene: Provide a specific setting, time period, or genre.
2. Introduce Characters: Describe the main characters and their motivations.
3. Define the Plot: Outline the main plot points and conflicts.

4. Specify the Tone and Style: Indicate the desired tone (e.g., humorous, serious, dramatic) and style (e.g., formal, informal, poetic).

Example:

Storytelling:

- Prompt: "Write a short story about a robot who dreams of becoming a chef. The robot should face challenges and overcome obstacles to achieve its dream."

Poetry:

- Prompt: "Write a haiku about the beauty of a sunset."

Script Writing:

- Prompt: "Write a short script for a comedy sketch about a person who is allergic to technology."

Code Example:

Python

```python
from transformers import pipeline


# Load a pre-trained text generation model

generator = pipeline("text-generation", model="gpt2")


# Prompt for a short story

prompt = "Write a short story about a robot who dreams of becoming a chef."
```

```
output = generator(prompt, max_length=200,
num_return_sequences=1)

print(output[0]['generated_text'])
```

Real-world Applications:

- Content Creation: Generating creative content for blogs, social media, and marketing materials.
- Education: Creating engaging stories and poems for language learning.
- Entertainment: Writing scripts for movies, TV shows, and video games.

By providing clear and inspiring prompts, you can encourage language models to generate creative and imaginative text.

Chapter 5: Implementing RAG Pipelines

5.1 Building a Basic RAG Pipeline

A basic RAG pipeline involves several key steps:

1. Document Collection and Preprocessing:
   - Gather Documents: Collect relevant documents from various sources (e.g., websites, PDFs, databases).
   - Clean and Preprocess: Clean the text by removing stop words, punctuation, and other irrelevant information.
   - Tokenization: Break down the text into tokens (words or subwords).
2. Document Embedding:
   - Choose an Embedding Model: Select a suitable embedding model (e.g., BERT, RoBERTa, Sentence-Transformers).
   - Generate Embeddings: Convert each document into a dense vector representation using the chosen embedding model.
3. Vector Database:
   - Create an Index: Create an index in a vector database (e.g., Faiss, Milvus, Pinecone) to store the document embeddings.
   - Insert Embeddings: Insert the document embeddings into the index, along with metadata (e.g., document title, source, URL).
4. Prompt Engineering:
   - Define the Task: Clearly articulate the task you want the language model to perform (e.g., question answering, text summarization).

- Craft the Prompt: Construct a well-defined prompt that includes the user's query and relevant context.
5. Language Model Processing:
    - Retrieve Relevant Documents: Use the vector database to retrieve the most relevant documents based on the query.
    - Process the Documents: Process the retrieved documents using a language model (e.g., GPT-3, Jurassic-1 Jumbo) to generate a response.

Code Example (Using LangChain):

Python

```python
from langchain.document_loaders import TextLoader

from langchain.embeddings import HuggingFaceEmbeddings

from langchain.vectorstores import FAISS

from langchain.chains import RetrievalQA


# Load documents

loader = TextLoader("documents.txt")

documents = loader.load()


# Create embeddings

embeddings = HuggingFaceEmbeddings()
```

```
db = FAISS.from_documents(documents, embeddings)


# Create a retrieval QA chain

qa_chain = RetrievalQA.from_chain_type(

    LLMChain(llm=OpenAI(model="text-davinci-003")),

    retriever=db.as_retriever()

)


# Ask a question

query = "What is the capital of France?"

response = qa_chain.run(query)

print(response)
```

Real-world Application:

A customer service chatbot can use a RAG pipeline to answer customer queries. The chatbot can retrieve relevant information from a knowledge base, process it using a language model, and generate informative and accurate responses.

By following these steps and leveraging the power of language models and vector databases, you can build effective RAG pipelines to solve a wide range of tasks.

Ingestion to Response Generation

Here's a step-by-step breakdown of building a basic RAG pipeline:

1. Data Ingestion and Preprocessing

- Gather Documents: Collect a diverse set of relevant documents, such as articles, reports, or books.
- Clean and Preprocess:
    - Remove noise like HTML tags, extra whitespace, and special characters.
    - Tokenize the text into words or subwords.
    - Apply techniques like stemming or lemmatization to reduce words to their root forms.

2. Document Embeddings

- Choose an Embedding Model: Select a pre-trained language model like BERT, RoBERTa, or Sentence-Transformers.
- Create Embeddings: Feed the preprocessed documents into the model to generate dense vector representations.

3. Vector Database

- Choose a Vector Database: Select a suitable vector database like Faiss, Milvus, or Pinecone.
- Index Embeddings: Create an index in the vector database to efficiently store and search the embeddings.
- Insert Embeddings: Insert the document embeddings and their corresponding metadata (e.g., title, source) into the index.

4. Prompt Engineering

- Define the Task: Clearly articulate the task you want the language model to perform (e.g., question answering, summarization).
- Craft the Prompt: Create a clear and concise prompt that includes the user's query and any relevant context.

5. Language Model Processing

- Retrieve Relevant Documents: Use the vector database to retrieve the most relevant documents based on the query.
- Process the Documents: Feed the retrieved documents and the prompt into the language model to generate a response.

Code Example (Using LangChain):

Python

```python
from langchain.document_loaders import TextLoader

from langchain.embeddings import HuggingFaceEmbeddings

from langchain.vectorstores import FAISS

from langchain.chains import RetrievalQA


# Load documents

loader = TextLoader("documents.txt")

documents = loader.load()


# Create embeddings

embeddings = HuggingFaceEmbeddings()

db = FAISS.from_documents(documents, embeddings)


# Create a retrieval QA chain
```

```
qa_chain = RetrievalQA.from_chain_type(

    LLMChain(llm=OpenAI(model="text-davinci-003")),

    retriever=db.as_retriever()

)


# Ask a question

query = "What is the capital of France?"

response = qa_chain.run(query)

print(response)
```

Real-world Application:

A customer service chatbot can leverage a RAG pipeline to provide accurate and informative answers to customer queries. The chatbot can retrieve relevant information from a knowledge base, process it using a language model, and generate a comprehensive response.

By following these steps and leveraging the power of language models and vector databases, you can build effective RAG pipelines to address a wide range of tasks and improve the performance of AI applications.

5.2 Advanced RAG Techniques

While the basic RAG pipeline provides a solid foundation, advanced techniques can further enhance the performance and capabilities of RAG systems.

1. Hybrid Search

- Combining Keyword Search and Semantic Search:
  - Keyword Search: Quickly identifies documents that contain specific keywords.
  - Semantic Search: Utilizes embeddings to find semantically similar documents, even if they don't contain exact keyword matches.
- Benefits:
  - Improved precision and recall.
  - Ability to handle complex queries and ambiguous terms.

2. Feedback Loops and Reinforcement Learning

- User Feedback: Incorporate user feedback to refine the RAG system's responses.
- Reinforcement Learning: Train the language model to generate responses that are more likely to be preferred by users.
- Benefits:
  - Continuous improvement of the system's performance.
  - Adaptation to user preferences and evolving information needs.

3. Contextual Understanding and Reasoning

- Contextual Awareness: The RAG system should be able to understand the context of a query and provide relevant responses.
- Reasoning Capabilities: The language model should be able to perform logical reasoning and draw inferences.
- Benefits:
  - More accurate and informative responses.
  - Ability to handle complex queries and generate creative content.

By incorporating these advanced techniques, RAG systems can deliver more sophisticated and effective results.

Would you like to delve deeper into any specific technique or explore additional advanced RAG concepts?

Hybrid search combines the strengths of both keyword-based search and semantic search to improve the accuracy and relevance of document retrieval in RAG systems.

Steps Involved:

1. Keyword-Based Search:
   - Tokenize the Query: Break down the query into individual words or tokens.
   - Search the Index: Use a traditional search engine or a vector database to find documents that contain the query terms.
2. Semantic Search:
   - Embed the Query: Convert the query into a dense vector representation using a language model.
   - Similarity Search: Compare the query embedding to the embeddings of documents in the vector database.
   - Retrieve Similar Documents: Identify documents that are semantically similar to the query, even if they don't contain exact keyword matches.
3. Combine Results:
   - Merge Results: Combine the results from keyword-based search and semantic search.
   - Rank Results: Rank the combined results based on relevance, considering factors like keyword match, semantic similarity, and document context.

Code Example (Using Faiss and Elasticsearch):

Python

```python
import faiss

from elasticsearch import Elasticsearch


# Create a Faiss index for semantic search

dimension = 768  # Dimension of embeddings

index = faiss.IndexFlatL2(dimension)

index.add(document_embeddings)


# Create an Elasticsearch index for keyword search

es = Elasticsearch()

es.index(index="my_index", body={"text": "This is a
sample document..."})


# Query the indexes

query = "What is the capital of France?"


# Keyword search

es_results = es.search(index="my_index", query=query)


# Semantic search
```

```
query_vector = model.encode([query])[0]

distances, indices = index.search(query_vector, k=5)


# Combine results

combined_results = es_results["hits"]["hits"] +
[{"_source": {"text": documents[i]}} for i in indices[0]]


# Rank results based on relevance

# ... (Implement ranking algorithm, e.g., using a
combination of keyword match score and semantic
similarity score)
```

Real-world Application:

A search engine can use hybrid search to improve search results.
For example, if a user searches for "climate change," the search
engine can use keyword search to find documents containing the
exact phrase and semantic search to find documents that discuss
related topics like global warming and environmental impact.

By combining keyword search and semantic search, RAG systems
can achieve more accurate and relevant results, especially for
complex and ambiguous queries.

Feedback loops and reinforcement learning are powerful
techniques to improve the performance of RAG systems. By
incorporating user feedback and training the model on reward
signals, RAG systems can adapt and learn over time.

Feedback Loops

Steps Involved:

1. User Interaction: Users interact with the RAG system and provide feedback on the quality of the generated responses.
2. Feedback Collection: The system collects user feedback, such as ratings, comments, or explicit feedback signals.
3. Model Update: The collected feedback is used to update the model's parameters or training data.

Example:

- User Query: "What is the capital of France?"
- RAG Response: "Paris"
- User Feedback: "Correct"
- Model Update: The model's confidence in the answer "Paris" for similar queries is increased.

Reinforcement Learning

Steps Involved:

1. Reward Function: Define a reward function that measures the quality of the generated response.
2. Policy Gradient Methods: Use algorithms like Policy Gradient to optimize the model's policy, which maps states to actions.
3. Training: Train the model to maximize the expected reward by iteratively generating responses and receiving feedback from the environment.

Example:

- Task: Generating product descriptions.
- Reward Function: Reward the model for generating descriptions that are accurate, informative, and persuasive.
- Training: Train the model on a dataset of product descriptions and their corresponding sales figures. The

model learns to generate descriptions that lead to higher sales.

Real-world Applications:

- Customer Service Chatbots: By analyzing user feedback, the chatbot can improve its responses over time.
- Language Models: Reinforcement learning can be used to fine-tune language models to generate more coherent and engaging text.
- Recommendation Systems: By incorporating user feedback, recommendation systems can provide more personalized and accurate recommendations.

By leveraging feedback loops and reinforcement learning, RAG systems can continuously improve their performance and provide more accurate and relevant responses.

Contextual understanding and reasoning are crucial for RAG systems to generate accurate and relevant responses. By considering the context of a query, RAG systems can provide more nuanced and informative answers.

Steps Involved:

1. Contextual Analysis:
   - Identify Relevant Context: Extract relevant information from the query and the retrieved documents.
   - Understand Relationships: Identify relationships between entities and concepts in the context.
2. Reasoning:
   - Logical Reasoning: Use logical rules and inferences to draw conclusions.
   - Causal Reasoning: Understand cause-and-effect relationships.

- Analogical Reasoning: Identify similarities and differences between concepts.
3. Response Generation:
   - Integrate Contextual Information: Incorporate the contextual understanding into the generation process.
   - Generate Coherent and Relevant Text: Generate text that is coherent, relevant, and addresses the query.

Example:

Query: "What is the best time to visit Paris?"

Contextual Understanding:

- Identify Relevant Factors: Consider factors like weather, tourist crowds, and cultural events.
- Understand Relationships: Recognize that the best time to visit Paris depends on the visitor's preferences and priorities.

Reasoning:

- Logical Reasoning: If the visitor prefers warm weather and fewer crowds, the best time to visit would be in the spring or fall.
- Causal Reasoning: If the visitor is interested in attending a specific cultural event, the best time to visit would coincide with the event.

Response Generation:

- Consider Context: Generate a response that takes into account the visitor's preferences and priorities.
- Provide Specific Recommendations: Suggest specific dates or time periods for the visit.

Real-world Applications:

- Customer Service Chatbots: Provide personalized recommendations based on customer history and preferences.
- Virtual Assistants: Assist users with complex tasks by understanding the context of the user's requests.
- Educational Tools: Generate personalized learning plans based on the student's knowledge level and learning style.

By improving contextual understanding and reasoning capabilities, RAG systems can provide more intelligent and helpful responses to user queries.

Part III

Applications of RAG in AI Systems

Chapter 6: RAG for Enhanced Search

6.1 Semantic Search: Beyond Keyword Matching

Semantic search is a technique that uses natural language processing to understand the meaning of a query and retrieve relevant information from a large dataset. Unlike traditional keyword-based search, semantic search goes beyond exact matches to find information that is semantically similar to the query.

How Semantic Search Works:

1. Text Embedding: Documents and queries are converted into dense vector representations, capturing their semantic meaning.
2. Similarity Search: The query vector is compared to the document vectors using similarity measures like cosine similarity or Euclidean distance.
3. Ranking: The most similar documents are ranked and returned as results.

Advantages of Semantic Search:

- Improved Accuracy: Semantic search can identify relevant documents even if they don't contain exact keywords.
- Better User Experience: It can understand the intent behind a query and provide more relevant results.
- Handling Ambiguous Queries: Semantic search can handle ambiguous queries by considering the context and intent.

Real-world Applications:

- Enterprise Search: Finding relevant documents within a company's internal knowledge base.
- E-commerce Search: Improving product search by understanding user intent.

- Academic Search: Finding relevant research papers based on semantic similarity.

RAG and Semantic Search:

RAG systems can leverage semantic search to improve the accuracy and relevance of document retrieval. By combining semantic search with language models, RAG systems can provide more informative and personalized responses.

Example:

Consider a user searching for "climate change effects on agriculture." A traditional keyword-based search might only return documents that contain these exact words. However, a semantic search engine could also return documents that discuss related topics like global warming, extreme weather events, and crop yields.

By understanding the semantic meaning of the query, semantic search can provide a more comprehensive and relevant set of results.

Building a Semantic Search Engine with RAG

Step-by-Step Guide

1. Data Preparation:

- Collect Documents: Gather a relevant dataset of documents (e.g., articles, research papers, FAQs).
- Preprocess Text: Clean the text by removing stop words, punctuation, and other irrelevant information.
- Tokenization: Break down the text into tokens (words or subwords).

2. Document Embedding:

- Choose an Embedding Model: Select a suitable embedding model like BERT, RoBERTa, or Sentence-Transformers.
- Create Embeddings: Embed each document into a dense vector representation.

3. Vector Database:

- Choose a Vector Database: Select a suitable vector database like Faiss, Milvus, or Pinecone.
- Index Embeddings: Index the document embeddings in the vector database.

4. Query Processing and Retrieval:

- Embed the Query: Embed the user's query into a dense vector representation.
- Similarity Search: Use the vector database to find the most similar documents to the query.
- Rank Results: Rank the retrieved documents based on their similarity to the query.

5. Language Model Processing (Optional):

- Contextual Understanding: If needed, use a language model to understand the context of the query and the retrieved documents.
- Response Generation: Generate a comprehensive and informative response based on the retrieved information.

Code Example (Using Haystack):

Python

```
from haystack import Pipeline

from haystack.nodes import EmbeddingEncoder,
FAISSDocumentStore
```

```python
# Create a document store

document_store =
FAISSDocumentStore(embedding_model="sentence-tra
nsformers/all-MiniLM-L6-v2")


# Load documents

document_store.add_documents([

    {"text": "This is the first document."},

    {"text": "This document is the second document."}

])


# Create a pipeline

pipeline = Pipeline()

pipeline.add_node(EmbeddingEncoder(model_name="s
entence-transformers/all-MiniLM-L6-v2"),
name="EmbeddingEncoder")

pipeline.add_node(document_store,
name="DocumentStore")

pipeline.add_node(Retriever(document_store=documen
t_store), name="Retriever")


# Query the pipeline
```

```
query = "What is the second document about?"

result = pipeline.run(query=query,
params={"Retriever": {"top_k": 1}})

print(result["answers"][0]["answer"])
```

Real-world Application:

A company can build a semantic search engine to help employees find relevant information within their internal knowledge base. For example, an employee can search for "best practices for customer support" and retrieve relevant articles, FAQs, and training materials.

By leveraging semantic search, RAG systems can provide more accurate and relevant information to users, improving productivity and decision-making.

Contextual search and personalized results are key features of advanced search engines. By considering the user's context, preferences, and past behavior, these search engines can provide more relevant and tailored results.

1. Contextual Search

Steps Involved:

1. Contextual Signal Extraction:
   - Identify relevant contextual information from the user's query, browsing history, or location.
   - Examples of contextual signals include:
     - User's location
     - Device type
     - Previous search queries

- Current webpage
  2. Query Refinement:
     - Use the extracted context to refine the search query.
     - Expand or narrow the search based on the user's intent.
  3. Semantic Search:
     - Use semantic search techniques to identify relevant documents based on their meaning and context.
  4. Result Ranking:
     - Rank the results based on their relevance to the query and the user's context.

Example:

A user searches for "best restaurants" on a mobile device while traveling in Paris. The search engine can use the user's location to identify restaurants in Paris and rank them based on factors like proximity, user reviews, and cuisine preferences.

2. Personalized Results

Steps Involved:

1. User Profile Building:
   - Collect information about the user's preferences, interests, and past behavior.
   - Use techniques like collaborative filtering and content-based filtering to build a user profile.
2. Personalized Search:
   - Tailor search results to the user's preferences and interests.
   - Rank results based on the user's past behavior and preferences.
3. Recommendation Systems:
   - Recommend relevant products, articles, or videos based on the user's profile and past behavior.

Example:

An e-commerce website can use personalized search to recommend products to users based on their browsing history and purchase history. For example, a user who frequently buys running shoes might be recommended new running shoe models or accessories.

Real-world Applications:

- E-commerce: Personalized product recommendations, tailored search results.
- Social Media: Personalized news feeds and content suggestions.
- Search Engines: Contextual search and personalized search results.

By incorporating contextual search and personalized results, RAG systems can provide a more tailored and engaging user experience.

Chapter 7: RAG for Content Generation

7.1 AI-Assisted Writing and Content Creation

AI-assisted writing and content creation is a powerful application of RAG systems that can significantly enhance productivity and creativity. By leveraging the capabilities of language models and document retrieval, AI can assist in various writing tasks, from generating ideas to producing polished content.

Key Applications:

1. Content Generation:
   - Blog Posts: Generate blog posts on a given topic, including outlines, introductions, and conclusions.
   - Social Media Content: Create engaging social media posts for platforms like Twitter, Instagram, and LinkedIn.
   - Marketing Copy: Write compelling marketing copy for product descriptions, ad campaigns, and email newsletters.
   - Creative Writing: Generate poems, short stories, and scripts.
2. Content Editing and Improvement:
   - Grammar and Style: Identify and correct grammatical errors and style inconsistencies.
   - Clarity and Conciseness: Improve the clarity and conciseness of the text.
   - Fact-Checking: Verify information and identify potential inaccuracies.
3. Idea Generation and Brainstorming:
   - Topic Suggestions: Generate ideas for blog posts, articles, or research papers.

- Brainstorming: Assist in brainstorming sessions by providing creative suggestions and alternative perspectives.

RAG Pipeline for Content Creation:

1. Prompt Engineering:
   - Define the desired output format and style.
   - Provide relevant context and guidelines.
2. Document Retrieval:
   - Retrieve relevant information from a knowledge base or external sources.
3. Language Model Processing:
   - Generate initial content based on the prompt and retrieved information.
   - Refine the generated content using feedback loops and iterative refinement.
4. Human Editing and Review:
   - Edit and refine the generated content to ensure quality and accuracy.
   - Add personal touch and unique insights.

By effectively leveraging RAG systems, writers can streamline their workflow, improve productivity, and generate high-quality content.

Product Descriptions

Prompt Engineering:

- Specific Product: "Write a concise and informative product description for a new wireless noise-canceling headphone."
- Detailed Product: "Write a detailed product description for a high-performance gaming laptop, highlighting its specifications, features, and target audience."

Blog Posts

Prompt Engineering:

- Topic-Based: "Write a blog post on the benefits of using AI in customer service."
- Keyword-Based: "Write a blog post targeting the keyword 'sustainable fashion,' focusing on eco-friendly clothing brands."
- Problem-Solution: "Write a blog post addressing the problem of slow website loading times and providing solutions."

Marketing Copy

Prompt Engineering:

- Ad Copy: "Write a persuasive ad copy for a new smartphone, emphasizing its camera features and battery life."
- Email Subject Line: "Write a compelling subject line for an email promoting a summer sale."
- Social Media Post: "Write a short and engaging social media post to announce a new product launch."

Code Example (Using Hugging Face Transformers):

Python

```python
from transformers import pipeline


# Load a pre-trained language model

generator = pipeline("text-generation", model="gpt2")
```

```
# Generate a product description

prompt = "Write a concise product description for a new
wireless noise-canceling headphone."

output = generator(prompt, max_length=100,
num_return_sequences=1)

print(output[0]['generated_text'])
```

Real-world Applications:

- E-commerce: Generating product descriptions for online stores.
- Digital Marketing: Creating blog posts, social media content, and email campaigns.
- Content Marketing: Producing high-quality content to attract and engage audiences.

By effectively leveraging RAG systems and prompt engineering techniques, businesses can streamline their content creation process and produce high-quality content at scale.

AI can be a powerful tool to enhance human creativity by providing inspiration, overcoming writer's block, and exploring new ideas.

Here are some ways AI can enhance human creativity:

1. Idea Generation

- Brainstorming Tool: Use AI to generate a list of potential topics, keywords, or themes.
- Creative Writing Prompts: Generate unique and inspiring writing prompts.

Example:

- Prompt: "Generate 10 creative writing prompts related to artificial intelligence."

2. Overcoming Writer's Block

- Sentence Completion: Use AI to complete sentences or paragraphs.
- Paragraph Generation: Generate new paragraphs based on a given topic or context.

Example:

- Prompt: "Write a paragraph about the ethical implications of AI."

3. Style and Tone Exploration

- Style Transfer: Experiment with different writing styles, such as formal, informal, humorous, or persuasive.
- Tone Adjustment: Adjust the tone of the text to match a specific audience or purpose.

Example:

- Prompt: "Rewrite the following text in a more humorous tone: 'The experiment failed.'"

4. Collaborative Writing

- Co-authoring: Collaborate with AI to write articles, scripts, or code.
- Feedback and Iteration: Use AI to provide feedback on drafts and suggest improvements.

Example:

- Prompt: "Write a short story about a robot who dreams of becoming a chef."

Tools and Techniques:

- Language Models: Use powerful language models like GPT-3 to generate creative text formats.
- Prompt Engineering: Craft effective prompts to guide the AI's output.
- Human-AI Collaboration: Work together with AI to enhance the creative process.

By leveraging AI as a creative tool, writers can overcome creative blocks, explore new ideas, and produce high-quality content.

Chapter 8: RAG for Knowledge Management and Question Answering

8.1 Building Corporate Knowledge Bases

A corporate knowledge base is a centralized repository of information that can be accessed by employees to improve decision-making, problem-solving, and productivity. RAG systems can significantly enhance the effectiveness of corporate knowledge bases by making information more accessible and searchable.

Key Steps in Building a Corporate Knowledge Base:

1. Identify Knowledge Sources:
   - Identify the key sources of information within the organization, such as documents, emails, and databases.
2. Data Extraction and Processing:
   - Extract relevant information from various sources.
   - Clean and preprocess the data to remove noise and inconsistencies.
3. Document Indexing:
   - Create a structured index of the documents, including metadata such as title, author, and keywords.
4. Embedding and Vector Database:
   - Convert documents into dense vector representations.
   - Store the embeddings in a vector database for efficient search.
5. RAG Pipeline:
   - Develop a RAG pipeline to process user queries, retrieve relevant documents, and generate concise and informative answers.

Benefits of RAG-Powered Knowledge Bases:

- Improved Search: Semantic search capabilities enable more accurate and relevant search results.
- Enhanced Knowledge Sharing: Facilitates knowledge sharing and collaboration among employees.
- Faster Problem-Solving: Quickly access relevant information to solve problems efficiently.
- Reduced Training Time: New employees can quickly learn about the organization and its processes.
- Increased Productivity: By providing easy access to information, RAG can boost productivity.

Real-world Example:

A large corporation can create a knowledge base that includes product documentation, customer support FAQs, and internal policies. Employees can use the knowledge base to find information about product specifications, troubleshooting procedures, and company guidelines.

By leveraging RAG, the company can ensure that employees have access to the most up-to-date and relevant information, leading to improved efficiency and customer satisfaction.

Knowledge Graph Construction

1. Define Entities and Relationships:

- Identify the key entities in your domain (e.g., people, products, organizations).
- Define the relationships between these entities (e.g., "works_for," "is_a_type_of," "located_in").

2. Data Extraction and Cleaning:

- Extract relevant information from various sources (e.g., databases, APIs, text documents).

- Clean and preprocess the data to ensure accuracy and consistency.

3. Knowledge Graph Creation:

- Triple Store: Represent entities and relationships as triples (subject, predicate, object).
- Graph Database: Use a graph database to store and query the knowledge graph.
- Knowledge Graph Framework: Utilize frameworks like Neo4j or RDFlib to build and manage the knowledge graph.

Example:

Consider a knowledge graph for a company's products.

- Entities: Product, Category, Customer
- Relationships: hasCategory, purchasedBy, isSimilarTo

Knowledge Graph Querying

1. Query Language:

- Cypher: A declarative query language used to query graph databases.
- SPARQL: A query language for RDF data.

2. Query Execution:

- Pattern Matching: Match patterns in the graph to answer queries.
- Path Finding: Find paths between nodes in the graph.
- Inference: Use logical reasoning to infer new information from the graph.

Example Cypher Query:

Cypher

```
MATCH (p:Product)<-[:hasCategory]-(c:Category)
```

```
WHERE c.name = "Electronics"

RETURN p.name, p.price
```

This query retrieves the names and prices of products in the "Electronics" category.

Real-world Application:

A pharmaceutical company can use a knowledge graph to track drug interactions, clinical trials, and patient data. This can help identify potential side effects, optimize treatment plans, and accelerate drug discovery.

Benefits of Knowledge Graphs:

- Improved Search: More accurate and relevant search results.
- Enhanced Decision Making: Better insights and decision-making capabilities.
- Data Integration: Integration of data from various sources.
- Semantic Search: Understanding the meaning of queries and providing contextually relevant information.

By building and querying knowledge graphs, organizations can unlock the value of their data and gain a competitive edge.

Real-time question answering systems leverage RAG to provide immediate and accurate answers to user queries.

Key Components:

1. Document Retrieval: Efficiently retrieve relevant documents from a large corpus.

2. Question Understanding: Analyze the user's query to identify the intent and key information.
3. Answer Generation: Generate a concise and informative answer based on the retrieved documents.
4. Real-time Response: Deliver the answer to the user promptly.

Step-by-Step Example:

1. User Query: "What is the capital of France?"

2. Document Retrieval:

- Embedding: Convert the query into a dense vector representation.
- Similarity Search: Search the vector database to find the most relevant documents containing information about France.

3. Question Understanding:

- Identify the key entity: "France"
- Identify the question intent: "Find the capital city"

4. Answer Generation:

- Extract Relevant Information: Extract information about the capital of France from the retrieved documents.
- Generate Response: Formulate a concise and informative response: "The capital of France is Paris."

Code Example (Using LangChain):

Python

```python
from langchain.document_loaders import TextLoader

from langchain.embeddings import HuggingFaceEmbeddings
```

```python
from langchain.vectorstores import FAISS

from langchain.chains import RetrievalQA


# Load documents

loader = TextLoader("documents.txt")

documents = loader.load()


# Create embeddings

embeddings = HuggingFaceEmbeddings()

db = FAISS.from_documents(documents, embeddings)


# Create a retrieval QA chain

qa_chain = RetrievalQA.from_chain_type(

    LLMChain(llm=OpenAI(model="text-davinci-003")),

    retriever=db.as_retriever()

)


# Ask a question

query = "What is the capital of France?"
```

```
response = qa_chain.run(query)

print(response)
```

Real-world Applications:

- Customer Service Chatbots: Provide immediate and accurate answers to customer inquiries.
- Virtual Assistants: Assist users with tasks and provide information.
- Search Engines: Enhance search results with real-time question answering capabilities.

Challenges and Considerations:

- Real-time Performance: Efficiently processing queries and retrieving relevant information.
- Contextual Understanding: Understanding the context of the query to provide accurate and relevant responses.
- Handling Ambiguous Queries: Disambiguating ambiguous queries to provide accurate answers.
- Ethical Considerations: Ensuring that the generated responses are unbiased and fair.

By addressing these challenges and leveraging advanced techniques, real-time question answering systems can provide a valuable tool for information access and decision-making.

Chapter 9: Ethical Considerations and Responsible AI

9.1 Bias and Fairness in RAG Systems

Bias in AI is a significant concern, particularly in systems that rely on large datasets and complex algorithms. RAG systems, which often leverage large language models, are susceptible to biases that can be reflected in their outputs.

Types of Bias:

1. Algorithmic Bias: This arises from the algorithms used to train and deploy the model. Biased algorithms can lead to discriminatory outcomes.
2. Data Bias: Bias in the training data can lead to biased models. If the training data is not representative of the real world, the model may make biased predictions.
3. Societal Bias: Societal biases can be reflected in the data and the model's outputs.

Mitigating Bias in RAG Systems:

1. Diverse and Representative Datasets: Use diverse and representative datasets to train the model.
2. Fairness Metrics: Employ fairness metrics to evaluate the model's performance across different groups.
3. Regular Bias Audits: Conduct regular audits to identify and address biases.
4. Transparency and Explainability: Make the model's decision-making process transparent to understand the reasons behind its outputs.
5. Human Oversight: Involve human experts to review and correct biased outputs.

Example:

A language model trained on a biased dataset might generate stereotypes or discriminatory language. For example, if the model is trained on a dataset that primarily features male authors, it may associate certain professions with specific genders.

To mitigate this bias, it is crucial to use diverse datasets that represent a wide range of perspectives and experiences. Additionally, regular audits and human oversight can help identify and correct biases in the model's output.

By addressing bias and fairness issues, we can ensure that RAG systems are used ethically and responsibly.

To mitigate bias in RAG systems, it's crucial to address biases in both the training data and the models themselves.

Mitigating Bias in Training Data

1. Data Collection and Curation:
   - Diverse Data Sources: Collect data from diverse sources to ensure a wide range of perspectives.
   - Data Cleaning and Preprocessing: Remove biases and inconsistencies in the data.
   - Data Augmentation: Augment the dataset with synthetic data to increase diversity.
2. Data Quality Assessment:
   - Identify Biases: Analyze the data for biases related to gender, race, age, or other factors.
   - Balance the Dataset: Ensure that the dataset is balanced and representative of the target population.

Mitigating Bias in Models

1. Fairness Metrics:

- Demographic Parity: Ensure that the model's predictions are distributed equally across different groups.
- Equalized Odds: Ensure that the model's false positive and false negative rates are equal across different groups.
- Calibration: Ensure that the model's predicted probabilities are calibrated across different groups.
2. Bias Mitigation Techniques:
    - Fairness Constraints: Incorporate fairness constraints into the model's training objective.
    - Adversarial Debiasing: Train a separate model to identify and mitigate bias in the main model's predictions.
    - Preprocessing Techniques: Apply techniques like reweighting or rebalancing to the training data.

Example:

If a language model is trained on a dataset that primarily features male authors, it may generate text that reinforces gender stereotypes. To mitigate this bias, we can:

- Collect a Diverse Dataset: Include works by female authors and authors from diverse backgrounds.
- Use Fairness Metrics: Evaluate the model's performance on a diverse set of examples to identify and address biases.
- Apply Adversarial Debiasing: Train a separate model to identify and correct biased outputs.

By carefully selecting and curating training data, and by employing appropriate bias mitigation techniques, we can develop more fair and equitable RAG systems.

9.2 Privacy and Security

Privacy and security are critical concerns when developing and deploying RAG systems. Protecting user data and preventing unauthorized access is essential to building trust and ensuring ethical AI practices.

Key Privacy and Security Considerations:

1. Data Privacy:
   - Data Minimization: Collect and store only the necessary data.
   - Data Anonymization and Pseudonymization: Mask or replace personally identifiable information.
   - Secure Data Storage: Implement robust security measures to protect sensitive data.
2. Model Security:
   - Secure Model Training: Protect model training data and prevent unauthorized access.
   - Model Access Control: Restrict access to the model to authorized personnel.
   - Model Watermarking: Add watermarks or signatures to the model to protect intellectual property.
3. User Privacy:
   - Transparent Data Collection: Clearly communicate data collection practices to users.
   - Secure Data Transmission: Encrypt data during transmission to prevent interception.
   - User Consent: Obtain explicit user consent for data collection and usage.

Real-world Challenges and Solutions:

- Data Breaches:
  - Implement robust security measures, such as firewalls, intrusion detection systems, and encryption.

- Regularly update security software and conduct security audits.
- Unauthorized Access:
  - Control access to sensitive data and systems.
  - Use strong authentication and authorization mechanisms.
- Model Theft:
  - Protect model intellectual property through legal measures and technical safeguards.
  - Watermark models to deter theft.

By addressing these privacy and security concerns, organizations can build trustworthy and ethical RAG systems that protect user data and maintain the integrity of the system.

Would you like to delve deeper into a specific aspect of privacy and security, such as data privacy regulations or model security best practices?

Protecting sensitive information is crucial in RAG pipelines, especially when dealing with personal data or proprietary information. Here are some key strategies to ensure data privacy and security:

1. Data Minimization

- Collect Only Necessary Data: Gather only the essential data required for the specific task.
- Avoid Overcollection: Refrain from collecting excessive data that may not be directly relevant.

Example: If building a chatbot to answer product queries, only collect necessary information like product ID, description, and customer reviews. Avoid collecting personal data like user names or addresses unless absolutely necessary.

2. Data Anonymization and Pseudonymization

- Anonymization: Remove personally identifiable information (PII) from the data.
- Pseudonymization: Replace PII with unique identifiers.

Code Example (Python):

Python

```python
import pandas as pd


# Sample DataFrame with sensitive information

df = pd.DataFrame({

    "name": ["Alice", "Bob", "Charlie"],

    "cmail": ["alice@example.com", "bob@example.com",
"charlie@example.com"],

    "age": [30, 25, 35]

})


# Anonymize the data by removing sensitive information

df_anonymized = df.drop(columns=["email"])


# Pseudonymize the names

df_anonymized["name"] = ["User1", "User2", "User3"]
```

```
print(df_anonymized)
```

3. Secure Data Storage and Transmission

- Encryption: Encrypt sensitive data both at rest and in transit.
- Secure Storage: Use secure storage solutions like encrypted databases and cloud storage with robust access controls.
- HTTPS: Use HTTPS to encrypt communication between the client and server.

4. Access Control

- Role-Based Access Control (RBAC): Grant access to sensitive data and systems only to authorized personnel.
- Least Privilege Principle: Grant users only the minimum necessary permissions.
- Regular Security Audits: Conduct regular security audits to identify and address vulnerabilities.

5. Model Security

- Model Watermarking: Embed a watermark or signature into the model to protect intellectual property.
- Model Access Control: Restrict access to the model and its training data.
- Secure Model Deployment: Deploy models in secure environments with appropriate security measures.

By implementing these strategies, organizations can build secure and privacy-preserving RAG systems that protect sensitive information and maintain user trust.

9.3 Responsible AI Practices

Responsible AI practices are essential to ensure that AI systems are developed and deployed ethically and responsibly. By following these practices, we can mitigate potential harms and maximize the benefits of AI.

Key Principles of Responsible AI:

1. Fairness: Ensure that AI systems are fair and unbiased.
2. Accountability: Hold developers and organizations accountable for the impacts of AI systems.
3. Transparency: Make AI systems transparent and understandable.
4. Privacy: Protect user privacy and data security.
5. Robustness: Develop AI systems that are robust and resilient to attacks.
6. Environmental Impact: Consider the environmental impact of AI, particularly in terms of energy consumption and carbon emissions.

Practical Guidelines:

1. Ethical Design:
   - Involve ethicists and social scientists in the development process.
   - Consider the potential societal impact of the AI system.
   - Design systems that are fair, unbiased, and inclusive.
2. Bias Mitigation:
   - Use diverse and representative datasets.
   - Monitor and mitigate bias in the model's outputs.
   - Employ fairness metrics to assess the model's performance.
3. Transparency and Explainability:
   - Develop techniques to explain the model's decision-making process.

    ○ Provide clear and understandable documentation.
4. User Privacy:
    ○ Obtain informed consent from users.
    ○ Minimize data collection and storage.
    ○ Implement strong security measures to protect user data.
5. Continuous Monitoring and Evaluation:
    ○ Monitor the performance of the AI system over time.
    ○ Identify and address potential issues.
    ○ Regularly update and improve the system.

By adhering to these principles and guidelines, we can develop AI systems that benefit society and minimize potential harm. It is crucial to foster a culture of responsible AI development, where ethical considerations are prioritized alongside technical excellence.

Transparency, accountability, and human oversight are essential for responsible AI development and deployment. By ensuring these principles, we can build trust and mitigate potential risks.

Transparency

- Model Interpretability: Develop techniques to understand the decision-making process of AI models.
- Feature Importance Analysis: Identify the most important features that influence the model's predictions.
- Visualization Tools: Use visualization tools to explain the model's behavior.

Accountability

- Ethical Guidelines: Establish clear ethical guidelines for AI development and deployment.
- Risk Assessment: Identify and assess potential risks and harms associated with the AI system.

- Auditing and Monitoring: Regularly monitor the performance of AI systems and identify potential biases or errors.

Human Oversight

- Human-in-the-Loop: Involve human experts in the development, deployment, and monitoring of AI systems.
- Continuous Evaluation: Regularly evaluate the performance of AI systems and make necessary adjustments.
- Ethical Review Boards: Establish ethical review boards to oversee AI development and deployment.

Real-world Example:

A healthcare AI system that diagnoses diseases should be transparent and accountable. The system should be able to explain its decisions to doctors, and human experts should review the system's diagnoses to ensure accuracy and fairness.

Code Example (Using LIME for Model Interpretability):

Python

```python
from lime import lime_tabular


# Create a simple machine learning model

model = ...


# Create a LIME explainer

explainer =
lime_tabular.LimeTabularExplainer(training_data,
```

```
feature_names=feature_names, class_names=['positive',
'negative'])


# Explain a prediction

explanation = explainer.explain_instance(instance,
model.predict_proba)

explanation.show_in_notebook(show_table=True,
show_all=False)
```

By prioritizing transparency, accountability, and human oversight,
we can develop AI systems that are safe, reliable, and beneficial to
society.

Part IV

Future Trends and Emerging Technologies

Chapter 10: The Future of RAG and Generative AI

10.1 Emerging Trends: Multimodal RAG, Generative Agents, and More

The future of RAG and generative AI is promising, with several exciting trends emerging:

Multimodal RAG

- Combining Text and Visual Information: Integrating text and image data to enhance understanding and response generation.
- Real-world Applications:
  - Visual Question Answering: Answering questions based on images and videos.
  - Image and Text Generation: Generating images based on text descriptions or generating text descriptions for images.

Generative Agents

- Realistic AI Characters: Creating AI agents that can interact with users in a natural and engaging way.
- Personalized Experiences: Tailoring interactions to individual users' preferences and needs.
- Virtual Assistants and Companions: Developing AI assistants that can provide companionship, support, and assistance.

Other Emerging Trends

- Neuro-symbolic AI: Combining neural networks with symbolic reasoning to improve model interpretability and reasoning capabilities.
- Reinforcement Learning from Human Feedback (RLHF): Training models to align with human values and preferences.
- Ethical AI: Developing AI systems that are fair, unbiased, and transparent.

By exploring these emerging trends, we can unlock the full potential of RAG and generative AI, leading to more innovative and impactful applications.

10.2 The Impact of RAG on Industries and Society

RAG has the potential to revolutionize various industries and significantly impact society. Here are some key areas where RAG can make a substantial difference:

Industry Impact

- Healthcare:
  - Medical Diagnosis: Assisting doctors in diagnosing diseases by analyzing medical records and symptoms.
  - Drug Discovery: Accelerating drug discovery by analyzing vast amounts of biomedical literature.
- Finance:
  - Fraud Detection: Identifying fraudulent transactions by analyzing financial data.
  - Risk Assessment: Assessing investment risks by analyzing market trends and economic indicators.
- Education:
  - Personalized Learning: Tailoring educational content to individual student needs.

- Intelligent Tutoring Systems: Providing personalized tutoring and support.
- Customer Service:
  - AI Chatbots: Providing 24/7 customer support and answering queries efficiently.
  - Sentiment Analysis: Analyzing customer feedback to improve products and services.

Societal Impact

- Increased Productivity: Automating routine tasks and improving efficiency.
- Enhanced Decision-Making: Providing data-driven insights and recommendations.
- Improved Accessibility: Making information accessible to a wider audience.
- Ethical Considerations: Raising concerns about job displacement, privacy, and bias.

Addressing Ethical Challenges:

To ensure the positive impact of RAG, it's crucial to address ethical challenges such as:

- Bias and Fairness: Develop algorithms to mitigate bias and ensure fairness in decision-making.
- Privacy: Protect user privacy and data security.
- Transparency: Make AI systems transparent and explainable.
- Job Displacement: Prepare for potential job displacement and create new opportunities.

By carefully considering these ethical implications, we can harness the power of RAG to create a better future for all.

10.3 Challenges and Opportunities in the Field

While RAG offers immense potential, it also presents several challenges and opportunities.

Challenges

- Data Quality and Quantity: The quality and quantity of training data significantly impact the performance of RAG systems.
- Model Bias: Biases in training data can lead to biased and unfair outputs.
- Ethical Considerations: Ensuring the ethical use of RAG systems, including issues of privacy, security, and fairness.
- Computational Cost: Training and deploying large-scale RAG systems can be computationally expensive.
- Interpretability: Understanding the decision-making process of complex models can be challenging.

Opportunities

- Enhanced Productivity: Automating tasks and improving efficiency.
- Improved Decision-Making: Providing data-driven insights and recommendations.
- Personalized Experiences: Tailoring experiences to individual users.
- New Business Opportunities: Creating innovative products and services based on RAG technology.
- Scientific Discovery: Accelerating scientific research by analyzing large datasets.

Addressing Challenges and Seizing Opportunities:

To overcome challenges and seize opportunities in the field of RAG, researchers and practitioners should:

- Focus on Data Quality: Invest in high-quality data and data cleaning techniques.
- Develop Robust Bias Mitigation Techniques: Employ techniques like fairness constraints, adversarial debiasing, and data augmentation.
- Prioritize Ethical Considerations: Adhere to ethical guidelines and conduct regular audits.
- Invest in Computational Resources: Utilize powerful hardware and cloud computing infrastructure.
- Foster Collaboration: Collaborate with experts from diverse fields to advance the field.

By addressing these challenges and capitalizing on the opportunities, we can unlock the full potential of RAG and shape a future where AI benefits society as a whole.

Appendix

A.1 Technical Deep Dive: Neural Search, Transformers, and Embedding Models

Neural Search

Neural search is a technique that leverages deep learning models to improve the accuracy and relevance of search results. Unlike traditional keyword-based search, neural search understands the semantic meaning of queries and documents, allowing for more nuanced and context-aware search.

Key Components of Neural Search:

1. Document Embedding: Documents are converted into dense vector representations that capture their semantic meaning.
2. Query Embedding: Queries are also converted into dense vector representations.
3. Similarity Search: The query vector is compared to the document vectors to find the most similar documents.
4. Ranking: The retrieved documents are ranked based on their similarity to the query.

Neural Search vs. Traditional Search:

- Traditional Search: Relies on keywords and exact matches.
- Neural Search: Understands the semantic meaning of queries and documents.

Transformers

Transformers are a type of neural network architecture that has revolutionized the field of natural language processing. They are highly effective for tasks like machine translation, text summarization, and question answering.

Key Components of Transformers:

1. Encoder-Decoder Architecture: The encoder processes the input sequence, and the decoder generates the output sequence.
2. Self-Attention: Allows the model to weigh the importance of different parts of the input sequence.
3. Multi-Head Attention: Multiple attention heads can capture different aspects of the input sequence.

Applications of Transformers:

- Language Models: GPT-3, BERT, and other large language models.
- Machine Translation: Translating text from one language to another.
- Text Summarization: Condensing long texts into shorter summaries.
- Question Answering: Answering questions based on a given context.

Embedding Models

Embedding models are used to represent words, phrases, or documents as dense vectors. These vectors capture the semantic and syntactic meaning of the text.

Types of Embedding Models:

1. Word Embeddings: Represent individual words as vectors.
2. Sentence Embeddings: Represent entire sentences as vectors.
3. Document Embeddings: Represent entire documents as vectors.

Popular Embedding Models:

- Word2Vec: A neural network model that learns word embeddings by predicting the context of a word.
- BERT: A powerful language model that can generate contextually relevant embeddings.
- Sentence-Transformers: A family of models specifically designed for sentence-level embeddings.

By understanding these advanced techniques, you can build more sophisticated and effective RAG systems.

A.2 Popular Tools and Frameworks for RAG

Several powerful tools and frameworks are available to build and deploy RAG systems. Here are some of the most popular ones:

LangChain

LangChain is a framework for building applications powered by language models. It provides a modular and flexible approach to creating RAG pipelines, including:

- Document Loaders: Load documents from various sources like PDFs, text files, or databases.
- Embeddings: Create embeddings for documents and queries.
- Vector Stores: Store and retrieve embeddings efficiently.
- Retrieval: Retrieve relevant documents based on user queries.
- Language Models: Interact with language models like GPT-3 or Hugging Face Transformers.
- Prompt Engineering: Create and refine prompts to guide the language model's responses.

Haystack

Haystack is an open-source framework for building question-answering systems and semantic search applications. It provides a range of components for building RAG pipelines, including:

- Document Store: Store and retrieve documents.
- Preprocessor: Preprocess documents for indexing and search.
- Retriever: Retrieve relevant documents based on user queries.
- Reader: Extract answers from the retrieved documents.
- Pipeline: Combine components to create end-to-end pipelines.

Other Notable Tools and Frameworks

- Hugging Face Transformers: A popular library for working with transformer-based models.
- FAISS: A library for efficient similarity search and clustering of dense vectors.
- Pinecone: A vector database for storing and retrieving embeddings.
- LangChainJS: A JavaScript library for building RAG applications in the browser.

Choosing the Right Tools:

The choice of tools and frameworks depends on your specific needs and expertise. Consider the following factors:

- Complexity of the task: For simple tasks, a lightweight framework like LangChain might suffice. For more complex tasks, a more comprehensive framework like Haystack may be necessary.
- Scalability: The ability to handle large datasets and complex queries.

- Customization: The flexibility to customize the pipeline to specific requirements.
- Community Support: The availability of documentation, tutorials, and a supportive community.

By leveraging these powerful tools and frameworks, you can build robust and effective RAG systems to solve a wide range of real-world problems.